I AM A SERVANT

Kim Huffman

authorHOUSE®

AuthorHouse™
1663 Liberty Drive
Bloomington, IN 47403
www.authorhouse.com
Phone: 1 (800) 839-8640

Scripture quotations marked NASB are taken from the New American Standard Bible®, Copyright © 1960, 1962, 1963, 1968, 1971, 1972, 1973, 1975, 1977, 1995 by The Lockman Foundation. Used by permission.

Published by AuthorHouse 08/25/2018

ISBN: 978-1-5462-5692-2 (sc)
ISBN: 978-1-5462-5691-5 (e)

Library of Congress Control Number: 2018910025

Print information available on the last page.

Contents

Dedication ix

Introduction. xi

1   "I Am A Servant" 1
    Mark 10:45 1

2   "One Mightier Than I". 6
    Mark 1:1-11 6

3   "The Holy One of God". 10
    Mark 1:14-28. 10

4   "We Have Never Seen Anything Like This". 15
    Mark 2: 1-12 15

5   "Doctor, Doctor" 19
    Mark 2:13-17. 19

6   "A New and Better Way" 23
    Mark 2:18-28 23

7   "Stretch Out Your Hand". 28
    Mark 3:1-6 28

8   "The Problem Of Popularity". 33
    Mark 3:7-19. 33

9   "Binding The Strong Man". 37
    Mark 3:20-27 37

10 "Behold, Your Mother and Your Brothers" 41
    Mark 3:28-35 41

11 "Making the WORD Produce" 45
    Mark 4:1-9 45

12 "The Kingdom of God" 50
   Mark 4:26-32 50

13 "Even the Wind and Sea Obey Him" 54
   Mark 4:35-41 54

14 "Turn Your Heart Toward Home" 59
   Mark 5:1-20 59

15 "No Laughing Matter!" 64
   Mark 5:35-43 64

16 "Shake Those Dirty Feet" 69
   Mark 6:7-13 69

17 "The Miracle Meal" 73
   Mark 6:30-44 73

18 A Walk on the Wild Side 78
   Mark 6:45-52 78

19 "The Heart of the Matter" 82
   Mark 7:14-23 82

20 "Some Crumbs for the Dogs" 86
   Mark 7:24-30 86

21 "The 9000 and 19 Full Baskets" 90
   Mark 8:14-21 90

22 "To the Unknown Servants" 95
   Mark 8:22-26 95

23 "Who Am I?" 99
   Mark 8:27-33 99

24 "The Secret of Following Jesus" 103
   Mark 8:34-38 103

25 "All Things are Possible" 107
   Mark 9:14-29 107

26 "Who is the Greatest?" 111
   Mark 9: 30-37 111

27 "For Better or For Worse" 115
   Mark 10:1-12 115

28 "Eternal Life Within Your Grasp"..........................120
    Mark 10:17-22...120

29 "The Leading Characteristic of a Leader"...................124
    Mark 10:35-45 124

30 "Have Mercy"..128
    Mark 10:46-52...128

31 "The Lord Has Need of It"...............................132
    Mark 11:1-11 132

32 "The Rejected Stone" 136
    Mark 12:1-12..136

33 "The Money Trap" 140
    Mark 12:13-17...140

34 "The Most Important Commandment" 144
    Mark 12:28-34 144

35 "Surplus or Sacrificial Giving?".........................148
    Mark 12:41-44 148

36 "Be on the Alert" 153
    Mark 13:14-37...153

37 "In Memory of Her".....................................157
    Mark 14:3-9 157

38 "Pressed Into Service"..................................161
    Mark 15:20-27 161

39 "Go Preach!"...165
    Mark 16:15,16 165

Epilogue...169

Dedication

This book is dedicated to my children and their spouses who have brought much joy into my life. Joy Gaye and Keith Jeremy were raised in the churches that I served as the preacher and were loved by those churches. Memories and knowledge my children gained from the churches I served is still with them and helping them today.

I would like to thank Deb Crothers for editing this book and correcting my mistakes. She said she loved doing it and from what I can tell she did an excellent job.

May this book be helpful to all who use it and may their walk be closer to our Lord and Savior because of this book. May each reader become a better servant for Jesus Christ.

Kim Huffman

Introduction

The Gospel of Mark is full of action. It tells us the things Jesus did. In this book there are 39 small group studies with discussion questions at the end of each study. These studies can be done individually or in a small group setting.

I. THE WRITER

It is widely held that the author of the gospel of Mark is John Mark. He was a cousin to Barnabas and accompanied Paul and Barnabas on a mission trip (Acts 12:25). Mark wrote about being with Jesus in the Garden of Gethsemane the night Jesus was arrested and tells of his escape from the Roman authorities naked.

II. THE DESTINATION AND DATE

Mark was a companion of Peter and was in Rome when Peter was preaching there in the mid 60's. As the gospel was spreading, there was a need for the gospel that had the Roman citizens in mind. The gospel of Mark was probably written when Peter was in jail in Rome or shortly after Peter's death. It seems that Mark was written before the destruction of the Temple in 70 AD, so a good date for the writing of Mark's gospel is 67 or 68 A. D.

III. PURPOSE

Mark was familiar with servants. He probably grew up in a home that had servants. Mark was a follower of Jesus who had learned the importance of being a servant for his Lord. Mark's gospel has as its main purpose to show Jesus Christ as a servant. Mark 10:45 says, "For even the Son of Man did not come to be served, but to serve, and to give His life a ransom for many." The key word of Mark is servant. Mark uses the word "immediately" 41 times to show us the actions of Jesus in his gospel.

It is my hope that as you work through this book you will become a better servant for Jesus Christ.

Chapter 1

"I Am A Servant"
Mark 10:45

"For even the Son of Man did not come to be served, but to serve, and to give His life as a ransom for many."

IF YOU TAKE "SERVE" OUT of "service" what do you have left? You just have "ice". There are many Christians who need to be defrosted. Many Christians have the right aim but they never get around to pulling the trigger. As we consider what it means to serve, I hope you will start pulling the trigger in some way.

"Servant" in the New Testament usually represents the Greek (doulos) which means bond slave. It can also mean (diakonos) which means deacon or minister. These two Greek words (doulos and diakonos) are synonyms. Both words denote someone who is not their own. They belong to the master that has purchased them. They are the master's property, bought to serve him at his beck and call. The slave's sole purpose is to do as he is told.

Christian service means, first and foremost, living out a slave relationship to one's Savior. 1 Cor. 6:19,20 says, "Or do you not know that your body is a temple of the Holy Spirit who is in you, whom you have from God and that you are not your own? For you have been bought with a price: therefore, glorify God in your body."

What work does Christ give us to do as His servants? We serve Him by becoming slaves to our fellow servants and by being willing to do literally anything, whatever the cost or however humbling it may be in order to help them.

That is what true love looks like. Jesus served the disciples when He washed their feet. This was a job for the lowest servant. When the New Testament talks about ministering to the saints, it is not talking about preaching. It is talking about giving ourselves, our time and our talents to help others in practical ways. The essence of Christian service is loyalty to our Lord and Savior, Jesus Christ. Only the Holy Spirit can create in us a desire to serve others in sympathetic and practical ways as we see and love people the way God does.

Exodus 21:1-6 says, "Now these are the ordinances which you are to set before them: ² If you buy a Hebrew slave, he shall serve for six years; but on the seventh he shall go out as a free man without payment. ³ If he comes alone, he shall go out alone; if he is the husband of a wife, then his wife shall go out with him. ⁴ If his master gives him a wife, and she bears him sons or daughters, the wife and her children shall belong to her master, and he shall go out alone. ⁵ But if the slave plainly says, 'I love my master, my wife and my children; I will not go out as a free man,' ⁶ then his master shall bring him to God, then he shall bring him to the door or the doorpost. And his master shall pierce his ear with an awl; and he shall serve him permanently."

These words give instructions and ordinances on how to treat slaves in light of Israel having just come out of slavery in Egypt. Understanding some of the basics about how slaves or servants were to be treated helps give us a general context for these lessons from Mark whose key word is "servant"

Being a Servant is a Choice

The choice was the Master's to buy someone as his slave "if" he wanted to do so (Exodus 21:2). Individuals could sell themselves as slaves if they wanted to do so. Often slaves were forced to sell themselves out of necessity, but it was their choice. Hard times, crop failure, famine, loss of possessions, or a debt that couldn't be repaid

often caused a person to choose to become a servant because there was no other option.

It is even probable that you could choose who you sold yourself to as a servant. Under these instructions you sold yourself for six years. Your Master would make payment ahead of time and settle your debt. The seventh year you were set free and your debt was considered paid in full.

The Conditions of Being a Servant

The terms of service were specific: six years. You were not a bond slave for life. This servanthood was nothing like what we understand slavery to be today. Masters were usually kind to their servants and bought them for six years to help them out of a jam. The Master gave the servant a home, food, clothing and they got the Sabbath off.

Selling yourself gave you a great deal of security in the midst of your insecurity, uncertainty and difficulties. It could even give you marriage and a family. The Master who bought you could, if he wanted to, give you a wife. However, she and any children you had belonged to the Master when you were freed the seventh year.

From Deuteronomy 15:12-18 it is clear that the Master had to give the freed servant food, flocks and wine proportionate to the blessing God gave the Master while the servant served the Master.

The Commitment of a Servant

When the seventh year came, the servant could decide to stay a servant of his Master or accept his freedom. If the servant chose freedom, he could only take his wife with him if he came with her unless the Master gave the wife to him that he took while a servant. The same applied to children.

No payment was given with the freedom. The Master was to give the freed slave some of his flock, crops and wine in proportion to how God had blessed him during the servant's service.

If the servant "plainly says" (Exodus 21:5) that he loves his Master, his wife and his children and wants to stay, he is allowed to do so if the Master brings him before God publicly. declaration of "love" was the servant's choice that he desired the loving relationship to continue.

The servant was required to make the public commitment to remain with the Master for the rest of his life. The outward sign of this commitment was having his ear placed against the city gate's door post and allowing the Master to put a hole in his ear with an awl. This became an outward witness of the servant's inward surrender to serve his Master.

This hole in the ear became a mark showing everyone that you were under the protection of your master and that you were important and of great value to him. It was a true mark of honor.

CONCLUSION

There are some important applications here for us today. Being a servant of Jesus Christ is our choice. It is a choice that should be for life. Being a servant of Jesus Christ offers us protection, security, hope and blessings we can find nowhere else. The blessing we are to our Master will come back to us as more blessings in our life. Serving Jesus Christ in this life will be rewarded with eternal freedom.

We must choose to love Christ as our Master and serve other people in our life. There should be a public display of our commitment to our Master. Our immersion into Christ can be that sign. We should live our life for our Master, Jesus Christ, so others know we belong to Him. When we serve our Master we will have hope, feel important and will have his blessings and protection.

During WWII, a church in Strasbourg, Germany, was destroyed by bombs. The members of this church, upon inspecting the remains, found the roof caved in and everything pretty much destroyed. They did discover that their statue of Christ with outstretched arms was intact except for its hands. Right away the people found the original sculptor and wanted him to carve new hands for Christ and attach them. He was willing and even would do it for free. All the details were taken to the congregation for a vote. The congregation decided against replacing the hands of Jesus on the statue. When asked why, the reasons were all the same. They felt that a statue without hands in the rebuilt church would be the best illustration possible that God's work is done through God's people. That is true. Jesus has chosen our hands to serve Him and others and finish the work He came to this earth to do. (Story adapted from Daily Devotional of Billy Graham Evangelistic Association)

Will you be a servant? Will you declare your love for the Master? Will you decide to make the commitment to serve the Lord for the rest of your life?

Discussion Questions

1. What does it mean to you to be a servant?

2. What does Exodus 21:1-6 show us about being a slave?

3. Why did people sell themselves into slavery sometimes?

4. What length of time would you be a slave?

5. How was a servant identified if they chose a life of servanthood?

6. What are some of the applications for us today from this study?

7. In what way will you try to be a better servant?

Chapter 2

"One Mightier Than I"
Mark 1:1-11

The beginning of the gospel of Jesus Christ, the Son of God.
² As it is written in Isaiah the prophet: "Behold, I send My
messenger ahead of You, who will prepare Your way; ³ the voice
of one crying in the wilderness, 'Make ready the way of the
Lord, make His paths straight.'" ⁴ John the Baptist appeared
in the wilderness preaching a baptism of repentance for the
forgiveness of sins. ⁵ And all the country of Judea was going
out to him, and all the people of Jerusalem; and they were
being baptized by him in the Jordan River, confessing their
sins. ⁶ John was clothed with camel's hair and wore a leather
belt around his waist, and his diet was locusts and wild honey.
⁷ And he was preaching, and saying, "After me One is coming
who is mightier than I, and I am not fit to stoop down and
untie the thong of His sandals. ⁸ I baptized you with water; but
He will baptize you with the Holy Spirit." ⁹ In those days Jesus
came from Nazareth in Galilee and was baptized by John in
the Jordan. ¹⁰ Immediately coming up out of the water, He
saw the heavens opening, and the Spirit like a dove descending
upon Him; ¹¹ and a voice came out of the heavens: "You are
My beloved Son, in You I am well-pleased."

INTRODUCTION

THE KEY WORD IN MARK'S gospel is SERVANT. Mark was written to a Roman audience and is a gospel of action. Mark uses the word "immediately" 41 times. Mark's emphasis is on what Jesus did rather than on what Jesus said. Mark refers to Jesus as "the Son of God" 9 times.

Mark's purpose for writing is best expressed in Mark 10:45, our theme verse in this study. I hope as we go through this study we will learn "to serve with love" one another in the church and the people outside the church.

Ten years from now, if we were to look back, what would some of the headlines be?

Here are some actual headlines from the newspaper from a few years ago:
- Include your children when baking cookies.
- Something went wrong in jet crash, experts say.
- Police begin campaign to rundown holiday jaywalkers.
- Drunk gets 9 months in violin case.
- Two sisters reunited after 18 years in checkout line.
- Man struck by lightning faces battery charge.
- Local high school dropouts cut in half. (From my files, author unknown)

I hope we can read a year from now, headlines like this:
- Church member lends helping hand to the needy.
- Sunday school class serves up help to homeless family.
- Congregation steps out in faith to better serve the community.

You could make up your own headlines that you want to see happen by next year.

Today's scripture tells us about John the Baptist. Let's look at his makeup, his message and his moment.

John the Baptist's Makeup

God had a plan and purpose for John, just like He does for each one of us. John had a purpose. It was to prepare the way for the Messiah, Jesus Christ. John's birth was special and in some ways was similar to Jesus' birth. John the Baptist fulfilled the prophecy of Isaiah (Mark 1:2, 3).

John the Baptist was a prophet that Jesus calls the greatest of all the prophets. John the Baptist preached in the wilderness and dressed the part and ate a strange diet. Perhaps this was a picture of Israel's wandering for 40 years.

John invited people to leave their wilderness experience and come to the Promised Land.

John's Message

He preached baptism unto repentance for the forgiveness of sins and that One mightier than he was coming (verse 4 and 7). The message of the need for baptism was new to the people, although it was practiced in other cultures. Thus, the people called John "the baptizer." Historical reports say that as many as 300,000 people may have come out to the Jordan River to be baptized by John.

John's message was not unlike the message of all the prophets - repent and turn to God. A servant must be willing to repent and turn to God. Matthew 14 tells of John the Baptist telling King Herod to repent because he had taken his brother Philip's wife (Herodias) and was living with her. We must be willing to tell people to repent and turn to God in a tactful way.

John's Moment

In the midst of John doing his ministry, Jesus came to be baptized by him. John 1:29 tells us that when John saw Jesus coming he said, "Behold, the Lamb of God who takes away the sins of the world". Jesus came to be baptized to fulfill all righteousness and not because He was a sinner (Matthew 3:14,15). John had prepared the way and he was humble enough to know that he was not even worthy to untie Jesus' sandals.

John baptized with water. Jesus would baptize with even more than water. He would also baptize with the Holy Spirit (Acts 2:38). Jesus was immersed, not sprinkled or poured. When Jesus came up out of the water, immediately the Spirit, in the form of a dove, descended on Him and the voice of God said, "This is my beloved Son, in whom I am well pleased" (Mark 1:10, 11).

What a moment for John! He got to baptize the Son of God, and he got to see the Holy Spirit descend in the form of a dove and he heard God's voice.

CONCLUSION

In John 3:29, 30, John the Baptist gives his final testimony about Jesus before he is put in prison and beheaded. He refers to Jesus as the bridegroom and himself as the friend of the bridegroom. He knew joy unspeakable because he had completed his God-given purpose. John the Baptist says that it was time for him to decrease and for Jesus to increase. We serve a God that is much bigger and mightier than we are. We need to let go and let God. As we go forward in our Christian life, may we realize that it is time to start serving others in Jesus' name. In that way Jesus will increase and we will decrease.

Discussion Questions

1. What is the key word in the gospel of Mark?

2. What are some of the characteristics that make Mark unique?

3. What does Jesus say about John the Baptist being a prophet?

4. What message did John the Baptist preach?

5. What did John the Baptist say when he saw Jesus coming?

6. When Jesus was baptized, what words did John the Baptist hear and what did he see?

7. How can we cause Jesus Christ to increase and ourselves to decrease?

Chapter 3

"The Holy One of God"
Mark 1:14-28

Now after John had been taken into custody, Jesus came into Galilee, preaching the gospel of God, [15] and saying, "The time is fulfilled, and the kingdom of God is at hand; repent and believe in the gospel." [16] As He was going along by the Sea of Galilee, He saw Simon and Andrew, the brother of Simon, casting a net in the sea; for they were fishermen. [17] And Jesus said to them, "Follow Me, and I will make you become fishers of men." [18] Immediately they left their nets and followed Him. [19] Going on a little farther, He saw James, the son of Zebedee, and John his brother, who were also in the boat mending the nets. [20] Immediately He called them; and they left their father Zebedee in the boat with the hired servants, and went away to follow Him. [21] They went into Capernaum; and immediately on the Sabbath He entered the synagogue and began to teach. [22] They were amazed at His teaching; for He was teaching them as one having authority, and not as the scribes. [23] Just then there was a man in their synagogue with an unclean spirit; and he cried out, [24] saying, "What business do we have with each other, Jesus of Nazareth? Have You come to destroy us? I know who You are — the Holy One of God!" [25] And Jesus rebuked him, saying, "Be quiet, and come out of him!" [26] Throwing him into convulsions, the unclean spirit cried out with a loud voice and came out of him. [27] They were all amazed, so that they debated among themselves, saying, "What is this? A new teaching with authority! He commands even the unclean spirits, and they obey Him." [28] Immediately the news about Him spread everywhere into all the surrounding district of Galilee.

INTRODUCTION

MARK INTRODUCED US TO JESUS through John the Baptist. He only spends two verses on Jesus' temptations in the wilderness (Mark 1:12, 13). In the text for this study, Mark shows us who Jesus really was. If you remember, Mark was not one to sit around. He liked action.

Larry Walters, 33, from San Pedro, CA, was just sitting around his house one weekend getting bored. He decided to do something adventurous. He went to an Army surplus store and bought 42 used weather balloons. Larry's plan was to fill the balloons with helium and strap them and himself to his lawn chair and float around the neighborhood at around 100 feet. Larry took along supplies, some sandwiches and a BB gun. Every once in a while, he planned to shoot a balloon and gradually he would descend back to the ground. (Really, I am not inflating this story. It appeared in the LA Times July 2, 1982).

There was just one hitch in Larry's plan. When the lawn chair left the ground, it didn't stop at 100 feet like Larry had planned. It soared to 16,000 feet, (a little over 3 miles up). Larry was spotted by a TWA pilot when he drifted into the landing pattern of LAX airport. Larry was getting cold. He managed to shoot a few of the balloons before he dropped the gun. There was no way he could let go of his death grip on the lawn chair. Eventually Larry drifted down to the backyard of a Long Beach home where he got hung up in some power lines. His chair was about five feet off the ground. He was able to free himself. Larry was arrested by police and fined $4,000.

A herd of reporters greeted Larry wanting to know why he would do such a thing. One reporter asked him if he was scared. (A brilliant question for a guy three miles up in the air in a lawn chair!) Another reporter asked Larry if he planned to do it again. "Nope," was his answer. And finally, a reporter asked the question everyone wanted to know: "What made you do such a thing in the first place?" Larry responded, "Well, sometimes you just can't sit there anymore." In other words, there comes a time when you just have to do something.

Jesus didn't just sit around. He was a servant. Let's look at what He did as we consider "The Holy One of God" from Mark 1:14-28.

The Holy One of God Went About Preaching the Gospel

Preaching the gospel of God was how Jesus served others (verse 14). Jesus said "the time is fulfilled" (verse 15) to begin His ministry. The kingdom of God was at hand (verse 15).

Jesus preached that people needed to repent and believe (put their trust in the Gospel) (verse 15). Immediately the news about Jesus went out everywhere into all the surrounding district of Galilee (verse 28).

The Holy One of God Called People to Follow Him

Simon (Peter) and Andrew, who were brothers and fishermen, followed Him (verses 16-18). They became fishers of men (verse 17). Verse 18 says they "immediately" left their nets and followed Him. Do you know how hard it is to get a fisherman to stop fishing?!

James and John, sons of Zebedee, were brothers who were called "sons of Thunder". They were fishermen mending their nets when Jesus called them to follow Him. James and John left their nets and their father in the boat to follow Jesus (verses 19, 20).

The Holy One of God Taught with Authority

Jesus took those who followed Him to the town of Capernaum. "Immediately" on the Sabbath, (when the people would come to the Synagogue), Jesus began to teach them (verse 21). The people were amazed at Jesus' teachings because He taught with authority which the Scribes didn't do (verse 22).

A man with an unclean spirit was there. Jesus cast the unclean spirit out the man. The unclean spirit knew who Jesus was. In verse 24 he cried out, "I know who you are - the Holy One of God!"

Jesus not only taught what was needed, He also served the needs that people had. This caused the people to debate this new teaching and authority that Jesus had because even unclean spirits obeyed Him (verse 27).

CONCLUSION

John the Baptist knew Him. Simon Peter and Andrew knew Him and followed Him. James and John left everything to follow Him. The people were amazed at His teaching and authority even debating among themselves who Jesus was. The unclean spirit knew who Jesus was - "The Holy One of God!"

But the real question is, "Who do you say He is?" Unless we see Jesus as the Holy One of God, we are probably not going to follow Him and obey His teachings. We probably won't share the message about Him with anyone and we for sure won't serve others in their need. Peter answered this question by saying in Matthew 16:16 - "You are the Christ, the Son of the living God."

Who is Jesus to you? Is He the Holy One of God? If He is then you just can't sit there! You have to get up and do something! You have to share the gospel, call others to follow Christ and trust His authority and teachings. What are you going to do?

Discussion Questions

1. What is the point of the story about Larry Walters, and how does it go along with Mark's story about Jesus?

2. What did Jesus preach?

3. In this lesson, who are the people Jesus called to follow Him?

4. What was different about the way Jesus taught?

5. Who did the man with the unclean spirit say Jesus was when he was healed?

6. Who do you say Jesus is?

7. What can you really do if you believe in Jesus?

Chapter 4

"We Have Never Seen Anything Like This"
Mark 2: 1-12

When He had come back to Capernaum several days afterward, it was heard that He was at home. [2] And many were gathered together, so that there was no longer room, not even near the door; and He was speaking the word to them. [3] And they *came, bringing to Him a paralytic, carried by four men. [4] Being unable to get to Him because of the crowd, they removed the roof above Him; and when they had dug an opening, they let down the pallet on which the paralytic was lying. [5] And Jesus seeing their faith *said to the paralytic, "Son, your sins are forgiven." [6] But some of the scribes were sitting there and reasoning in their hearts, [7] "Why does this man speak that way? He is blaspheming; who can forgive sins but God alone?" [8] Immediately Jesus, aware in His spirit that they were reasoning that way within themselves, *said to them, "Why are you reasoning about these things in your hearts? [9] Which is easier, to say to the paralytic, 'Your sins are forgiven'; or to say, 'Get up, and pick up your pallet and walk'? [10] But so that you may know that the Son of Man has authority on earth to forgive sins" —He *said to the paralytic, [11] "I say to you, get up, pick up your pallet and go home." [12] And he got up and immediately picked up the pallet and went out in the sight of everyone, so that *they were all amazed and were glorifying God, saying, "We have never seen anything like this."*

INTRODUCTION

THE HEALING OF THE PARALYZED man in this text was the occasion Jesus chose to demonstrate why He came. Jesus was a great healer. There is no question about that. But what is the spiritual lesson He wanted us to see in this healing? In Some ways it is a mystery that He wants us to carefully consider.

Here are a few mysteries of anatomy to ponder:

Where can a woman buy a cap for her knee or the key to a lock of her hair? Is the crown of your head where jewels are found? No wonder it hurts when a woman gives birth. Who travels across the bridge of your nose? If you wanted to shingle the roof of your mouth would you use the nails from your fingers and toes? Can you sit in the shade of the palm of your hand? Can you beat on the drum in your ear? Can the calf of your leg eat the corn on your foot? Why isn't there corn on your ear? Can the crook of your elbow be sent to jail? If so, would the charge be armed robbery? How can you sharpen your shoulder blades? Where are the eyes in your eye teeth? If Solomon's temple was on the side of his head why do we say it was in Jerusalem?

Jesus did amazing things. In fact, people were saying, "We have never seen anything like this." In this lesson we want to look at some characteristics of some real characters.

The Characteristics of the Four Friends

They had a great love. They were concerned enough about their friend that they did something. They didn't just talk about it.

They had a great faith. They believed that Jesus could heal their paralyzed friend.

They have even had a great prayer life. But they didn't just pray. They put feet on their prayers.

They had a great persistence. They were not easily discouraged by difficult circumstances when the house was full and there was no room to go in.

They had great teamwork. They worked well together to complete the task. They each did their part and did what they could.

The Characteristics of the Critics

The Scribes and Pharisees reasoned in their hearts that only God could forgive sins. That was true. But these critics did not have open minds. They accused Jesus of blasphemy. They would have been more concerned about the hole in the roof than about the man who was healed. They were indifferent and just sitting there, verse 6 says.

Luke 5:17 tells us that these critics were just there to spy on Jesus and were looking for something they could use against Him. They probably even came early to get the best seats.

This is the beginning of the opposition to Jesus that eventually caused Him to go to the cross.

The Character of Jesus

Jesus was at Peter's house and was speaking the Word of God to those who had gathered there. Jesus had a following of people who had heard about the things He was doing and saying. So many people came that there was no more room (verse 2).

Jesus saw the faith of the four men and rewarded their faith (verse 5). Interestingly Jesus forgave the man's sins rather than healing him. Jesus saw the real need in this man when all the people only saw the outside need of the man. It is true that Jesus looks on the inside of us to see our hearts.

Jesus claimed to be God, and so to prove it He healed the man (verse 10-12). Mark uses the term "Son of Man" 14 times. This title was a Messianic one (Daniel 7:13, 14) that the Jews would have understood.

CONCLUSION

Jesus healed this paralyzed man to teach the spiritual lesson that He was God. Only God can forgive sins. Healing the man's physical body was an outward demonstration that Jesus had the power to heal the man's soul. He cleared up any mystery as to whether He could forgive sins by healing the man. The Scribes and Pharisees had reasoned that only God can forgive sins. They were completely right. All Jesus did was show them that he was the "Son of Man" by healing the paralyzed man. Sin is a sickness. The forgiveness of sin is a healing that is even better than a physical healing.

Carl Michalson tells about the time he was playing with his young son. They were rough housing around and he accidentally hit his son in the face with his elbow. The impact was hard enough that he knew it had to hurt. His son was about to burst into tears from the pain when he looked into his father's eyes. Instead of anger and hostility the young son saw sympathy, anguish and concern. He saw love and compassion in his father's eyes. Instead of bursting into tears he began to laugh. It was what he saw in his father's eyes that made all the difference.

The sharp blow of God's message is the call to repent. And we look into the Father's eyes and we see Him offering us forgiveness for our sins. That makes all the difference in the world to us.

If you have not done anything about your sins, Jesus will meet you and forgive them for you. You can wash them all away.

I tell you the truth. I have never seen anyone like that but Jesus.

Discussion Questions

1. What did Jesus hope to show by healing the paralyzed man in this lesson?

2. What was the reaction of the people when they saw this man healed?

3. What do you like best about the four friends?

4. Why were the Scribes and Pharisees at this house?

5. What did Jesus do before He healed this paralyzed man and why did He do it?

6. What name does Mark use for Jesus 14 times?

7. Why do you think Jesus came according to this lesson?

Chapter 5

"Doctor, Doctor"
Mark 2:13-17

And He went out again by the seashore; and all the people were coming to Him, and He was teaching them. ¹⁴ As He passed by, He saw Levi, the son of Alphaeus, sitting in the tax booth, and He *said to him, "Follow Me!" And he got up and followed Him. ¹⁵ And it happened that He was reclining at the table in his house, and many tax collectors and sinners were dining with Jesus and His disciples; for there were many of them, and they were following Him. ¹⁶ When the scribes of the Pharisees saw that He was eating with the sinners and tax collectors, they said to His disciples, "Why is He eating and drinking with tax collectors and sinners?" ¹⁷ And hearing this, Jesus said to them, "It is not those who are healthy who need a physician, but those who are sick; I did not come to call the righteous, but sinners."

INTRODUCTION

JESUS IS SOMETIMES CALLED THE great physician. This is because of the power He had to heal people. I think Jesus also had a great bedside manner. That is truly a mark of a good servant.

This text is about the calling of Levi, (Matthew), a tax collector. If you were a Jew living in Capernaum during Jesus ministry you would have been under Roman rule and would have been required to pay taxes. There was a poll tax that was for the maintenance of the Temple. Every male between 14-65 and every female between 12-65 was required to pay a half shekel which amounted to about a half days wages. There was also a ground tax. This amounted to one tenth of the grain that you harvested and one fifth of your wine and oil. There was also a similar tax on fish that you caught. On top of that there was an income tax that you had to pay which was one percent of your annual income. The tax collector didn't get any of this money. The tax collector, however, had the power to stop anyone at any time and collect a duty tax on your possessions (wagons, carts, animals, clothing etc.). This is the way a tax collector got rich.

Of all the people the Jews loved to hate, tax collectors were at the top of their lists. Of all the people who lived at Capernaum, Levi, (Matthew), was the least likely to become a disciple. Our text tells us that as Jesus was leaving Capernaum and walking back out to the Sea of Galilee, He took the street that passed by where Levi's tax office was. Levi was sitting there possibly doing some accounting or planning where he would collect his next duty tax.

What takes place between Jesus and Levi is the heart of the Gospel. What happened could also happen to us, so let's look at it.

The Decisive Act

Jesus called Levi to follow Him just like he had called Peter, Andrew, James and John (verse 14). Levi rose and followed Him. Luke 5:28 adds that "Levi left everything behind and rose up and began to follow Him." While everyone saw Levi as "scum of the earth", Jesus saw great potential in him.

Levi's name was changed to Matthew, which means "gift of God".

The Dinner Party

The change in Matthew was so dramatic that he threw a big reception, banquet party to celebrate and Jesus was his special guest (verse 15). Some of the other guests, besides Jesus and His disciples, were Matthew's tax collector buddies and sinners.

The Scribes and Pharisees saw all this and asked, "Why is Jesus eating and drinking with tax collectors and sinners?" (verse 16). Many of these tax collectors and sinners were following Jesus too.

Matthew, who had no training in evangelism or calling techniques, wanted to introduce his friends to Jesus. So, he just got them together and started telling them about Him. Luke wasn't talking about Matthew in Luke 15:32 but it sure applies to him - "We had to rejoice because that which was lost has been found."

The Doctor's Cure

Dr. Jesus saw Matthew's friends not as sinners but as patients who needed healing. He answered the Scribes and Pharisees by saying, "It is not those who are healthy who need a physician, but those who are sick. I did not come to call the righteous but sinners" (verse 17).

Dr. Jesus sees our need and meets it. He always makes the proper diagnosis and provides the perfect cure. Dr. Jesus wants us to look for people who we can serve. We may not have the same power to meet their needs like Jesus did but we can introduce them to Him. Dr. Jesus pays our bill in full.

CONCLUSION

There are three kinds of patients that Dr. Jesus can't cure: those who don't know Him, those that know Him but refuse to take the medicine He prescribes, and those who will not admit they need His help.

It is not the healthy who need the Doctor but the sick. Jesus came to treat sinners. We cannot isolate ourselves from the people who are sick. We must go to them and meet their needs and help them get well by offering them the gospel medicine.

Walter Knight tells this true story: "Dr. Howard Kelly was a noted Dr. and surgeon who was a Christian. During his medical school days, he put himself through school by selling books door to door. On one particularly hot summer day Dr. Kelly became very thirsty. He approached a farm house, knocked on the door and asked for a drink of water. A girl came to the door. She sweetly offered Dr. Kelly a cold refreshing glass of milk. The years passed and Dr. Kelly graduated from medical school. He became the chief surgeon at John Hopkins Hospital.

One day, a patient was admitted to the hospital. She was from a rural area and was very sick. She was given special care and the surgery she needed to make her well. After the surgery she made a speedy recovery. The day came that the head nurse told her she could go home. Her joy was great but it was lessened by the thought of the large hospital bill she would have to pay since she had no insurance. She asked for a copy of her bill. She closely read each entry of her bill from top to bottom. But as her eyes reached the last line she couldn't believe what she saw. It said, "Paid in full with one glass of cold refreshing milk!" It was signed, Howard Kelly, MD. Jesus Christ is the Great Physician. He has a cure for you if you accept it!

Discussion Questions

1. Why is Jesus called the great physician?

2. What was Levi's name changed to and what does it mean?

3. Why would Jesus want someone like Levi to follow Him?

4. Who did Jesus say needed a doctor?

5. What medicine does the lost need?

6. How did Matthew tell others about Jesus without taking a class in personal evangelism?

7. Who can't the doctor cure?

Chapter 6

"A New and Better Way"
Mark 2:18-28

John's disciples and the Pharisees were fasting; and they came and said to Him, "Why do John's disciples and the disciples of the Pharisees fast, but Your disciples do not fast?" ¹⁹ And Jesus said to them, "While the bridegroom is with them, the attendants of the bridegroom cannot fast, can they? So long as they have the bridegroom with them, they cannot fast. ²⁰ But the day will come when the bridegroom is taken away from them, and then they will fast in that day.

²¹ "No one sews a patch of unshrunk cloth on an old garment; otherwise the patch pulls away from it, the new from the old, and a worse tear results. ²² No one puts new wine into old wineskins; otherwise the wine will burst the skins, and the wine is lost and the skins as well; but one puts new wine into fresh wineskins."

²³ And it happened that He was passing through the grain fields on the Sabbath, and His disciples began to make their way along while picking the heads of grain. ²⁴ The Pharisees were saying to Him, "Look, why are they doing what is not lawful on the Sabbath?" ²⁵ And He said to them, "Have you never read what David did when he was in need and he and his companions became hungry; ²⁶ how he entered the house of God in the time of

Abiathar the high priest, and ate the consecrated bread, which is not lawful for anyone to eat except the priests, and he also gave it to those who were with him?" [27] Jesus said to them, "The Sabbath was made for man, and not man for the Sabbath. [28] So the Son of Man is Lord even of the Sabbath."

INTRODUCTION

MARK HAS BEEN SHOWING US that Jesus came to be a servant and to seek and save the lost. Jesus is an example worthy of following because He is the "Son of Man." He wants to show us a new and better way to live.

I am old enough that I can remember some new and better ways of doing things. I can remember on the farm when we got a pipe line for the milking parlor so we didn't have to keep carrying the heavy canisters of milk. I remember the days before computers, email, and cell phones. I am not old enough like some of you who can remember that transportation was by horse and the bathroom was out back. I have only known the new and better ways of the gasoline engine and inside plumbing. Even many of the things that we now know as modern conveniences will one day be outdated and replaced by new and better things.

The point is this: when new and more modern things come along that makes life easier and better, it is foolish not to embrace those things. How many farmers would go back to farming with horses? How many number crunchers would give up their computers and calculators to do accounting with a pencil and paper? What teenager would give up the phone, texting and online chatting for letter writing?

This text tells us that Jesus came to show us a new and better way. To make His point Jesus talks about fasting, new and old clothing, wineskins and the Sabbath.

The New and Better Way Calls for Commitment

John the Baptist and the Pharisee's disciples fasted, but Jesus' disciples didn't. The OT law required fasting once a year on the Day of Atonement. The Pharisees had made up rules that said you had to fast on Monday and Thursday each week.

Jesus said that you don't fast as long as the Bridegroom is with you. John the Baptist had called Jesus the Bridegroom in John 3:28-30. The Pharisees even had a law that wedding guests were excused from religious observances that would lessen the joy of the wedding.

Jesus was implying that a wedding should be celebrated, not mourned. When we become a Christian, we die to the law and are married to Christ (Romans 7:4).

Jesus asks us to make a commitment to Him and follow and obey Him because He is the new and better way.

The New and Better Way calls for a Change

The religious leaders of Jesus day were content to add and make subtle changes to the old religious system. They were more interested in compromise than new and better. Jesus came to usher out the old and bring in the new. Matthew 5:17 says that Jesus came not to do away with the old but to fulfill it. Luke 22:19, 20 tells us that the bread and the cup of the Lord's Supper are a reminder of the new covenant in his blood.

There are two ways to destroy something: you can smash it or you can allow it to fulfill itself. An acorn can be smashed with a hammer or it can be planted and allowed to grow into an oak tree. In both ways the destruction of the acorn is complete. In the second way the acorn may be gone but it has changed into something even better.

Jesus is saying that He has fulfilled the OT and brought something even better. It is truly sad when people hold onto old dead religions and traditions when a new and better way is available. Jesus used the new patch on an old garment and old wine skins and new wine skins to illustrate the danger of not changing.

When we become Christians the old passes away and we become new. 2 Corinthians 5:17 says, "If anyone is in Christ, they are a new creature; the old things have passed away and new things have come."

The New and Better Way Creates Collisions

The problem was that the religious leaders had wrong priorities. They had made so many rules and regulations and those rules and regulations had become more important than people. As an example, there were 39 things that you could not do on the Sabbath.

Jesus saw people as being more important than rules. Rules are important but they are not more important than people. That is why Jesus allowed the disciples to take grain and eat it on the Sabbath and why He healed people on the Sabbath.

Keeping the Sabbath had become a real burden. It was not illegal to take some grain on the Sabbath and eat it, but the religious leaders saw what the disciples did as work and that was illegal. What the disciples did was not breaking the law. It was breaking the man-made traditions the religious leaders had created. Jesus even cited David's eating of the show bread on the Sabbath in the temple. Clearly Jesus is saying that people are more important than rules. Rules should be obeyed, but there are times when people are more important than the rules.

Jesus' point was that the Sabbath was made for man, not man made for the Sabbath.

CONCLUSION

Jesus came as a servant offering people forgiveness from their sins and a new and better way. Some followed Him and some chose to continue in their old ways.

In the April 1997 issue of Guidepost, Elizabeth Sherrill tells about a time she was working at her computer when she saw a strange sight out her window. She saw a skunk stumbling across her yard wearing a yellow helmet. At least it looked like a yellow helmet. It really was a yellow yogurt container that was stuck on his head. She called the DNR but was told she would have to pull the container off the skunk's head herself as the DNR didn't have personnel for things like that. "But what if it sprays me?" she asked. The man on the phone told her the skunk won't spray you if he can't see you. Elizabeth responded, "OK, but what happens once I pull off the container?" Mr. DNR said, "Just make sure he doesn't feel threatened."

She thanked the man weakly and hung up the phone. She put on a jacket and went outside to look for the skunk. The skunk was nowhere to be found. She was a little relieved until she saw a black and white stripe coming right toward her as she was about to go back inside the house. As the skunk came near she forgot about the implications and stooped down to pull the yogurt container off the skunk's head. Suddenly, Elizabeth found herself staring into two alert little black eyes only two feet away from her. She held the skunks gaze for a few seconds before he turned and ran, disappearing into a nearby culvert.

Often we are too afraid to pull off the yogurt container. We would rather just leave things the way they are. We don't want to get involved. We are too afraid of what might happen if we do. After all, it is not our fault that skunks get into trouble. But when we get involved, we can make a difference. Sure, there are risks and dangers. But a new and better way may just be available. Jesus offered people a new and better way. He offers forgiveness and a chance to start over. He offers a new and better way! Will you choose it?

Discussion Questions

1. Jesus came to show us what?

2. Why didn't Jesus make the disciples fast?

3. What does the new and better way ask of us?

4. What are the two ways you can destroy something?

5. How did Jesus bring a new and better way?

6. What view did Jesus and the religious leaders have about rules and people?

7. How will you get involved to make a difference in someone's life?

Chapter 7

"Stretch Out Your Hand"
Mark 3:1-6

He entered again into a synagogue; and a man was there whose hand was withered. 2 They were watching Him to see if He would heal him on the Sabbath, so that they might accuse Him. 3 He said to the man with the withered hand, "Get up and come forward!" 4 And He said to them, "Is it lawful to do good or to do harm on the Sabbath, to save a life or to kill?" But they kept silent. 5 After looking around at them with anger, grieved at their hardness of heart, He said to the man, "Stretch out your hand." And he stretched it out, and his hand was restored. 6 The Pharisees went out and immediately began conspiring with the Herodians against Him, as to how they might destroy Him.

INTRODUCTION

DO YOU HAVE TROUBLE COMMUNICATING sometimes? Here are some people who had trouble communicating in their newspaper ads.

"Antique desk 4 sale, suitable for lady with thick legs & large drawers."

"Earring special - have your ears pierced and get an extra pair to take home free."

"Illiterate? Write today for free material."

"Dry cleaners - we never tear your clothes with machinery, we do it carefully by hand."

"Help wanted in dynamite factory, must be willing to travel."

"Professional mixing bowl set for sale, perfect for lady with round bottom suitable for beating."

From Mark 3:1-6, I hope to communicate to you some very important information about going to worship. From what Mark has already told us, we know Jesus and the religious leaders were not seeing eye to eye on spiritual matters. In this text the Pharisees were watching Jesus to find something they could use to accuse Him (verse 2). It wasn't hard for these religious leaders to find Jesus. It was the Sabbath and Jesus was in the Synagogue. On the Lord's Day do people know where you will be?

Jesus was in the midst of many worshippers who had come to the Synagogue. Let's see what we can learn from them that will help us in our gathering together for worship.

THOSE WHO WERE "AT" WORSHIP

I say "at" worship because we can come to a worship service but never really worship. There were four different worshippers-

"Jesus" was at worship. We go to worship because of Jesus. If Jesus is not at worship where we go. then it is a waste of time.

"They" (verse ?) refers to the Pharisees and the religious leaders of the Jews.

"Unnamed worshippers" were there but we are not told how many were at worship. But we know there had to be at least ten men to have a Synagogue there.

"The man with the withered hand" (verse 1 and Luke 6:6) was there to worship. Some say he was probably planted in the worship service by the religious leaders. But the text doesn't say that. It seems from the text that he was just one of the worshippers.

THE ATTITUDE OF THOSE "AT" WORSHIP

"Jesus'" custom was to be in the Synagogue on the Sabbath (Luke 4:16). Mark 1:21 tells us that Jesus went into the Synagogue and began to teach. This was His custom. Mark 1:39 adds that Jesus went into the Synagogues throughout Galilee preaching & casting out demons.

"The religious leaders" were "at" worship but they were not worshiping. They appear as spectators. Their real reason for being there was to gather evidence against Jesus. They were watching Jesus to see if He would heal the man with the withered hand. They were not there for a spiritual purpose. They kept silent because they couldn't reveal themselves or their plan.

"Unnamed worshippers" were there but we don't know how many. Some of them had come to worship for the right reason and some had probably come for the wrong reason.

"The man with the withered hand" in this text may not have been born that way. He possibly had an accident or illness that caused his hand to be useless. He was there to worship. Nothing in the text indicates that he was there to be healed. But he became the center of attention when Jesus said to him, "Rise and come forward, stretch out your hand." He became a willing participant. Jesus called the man forward because He wanted everyone to have compassion for this man.

LESSONS LEARNED AT WORSHIP

There are some lessons we can learn from this text. People are going to come to worship for many reasons. Some of their reasons are good and some are bad. We must ask ourselves, "Why am I here at worship? Am I here for the right reason?"

Jesus is angry (verse 5) at those who are "at" worship for the wrong reasons. The word that is used here for "looking around" means to look around at each one with eye to eye contact. The Lord knows why we are at worship. It had better be for the right reason.

If we want to get something out of worship we have to participate. An old-time preacher used to say, "When you go to the spring for water, you've got to take your bucket." Some come to worship with a sieve and some come with buckets that are full of holes. Some come to the well and they don't bring a bucket at all. When you come to worship, what do you bring? The man with the withered hand brought a willingness to obey.

What we do with the truth is important. The religious leaders kept silent (verse 4). They had to because they knew that it was lawful to do good on the Sabbath. They knew that on the Sabbath it was lawful to save a life rather than kill one. But they went out of the Synagogue (verse 6) and began plotting to kill Jesus with the Herodians (a group of Jews loyal to Herod that supported Roman rule).

When we miss church, we miss the chance for a real blessing. What if the man with the withered hand had not bothered to go to worship? And what if he would have refused to come forward and stretch out his hand?

CONCLUSION

Why do you go to worship? Henry Ward Beecher was a famous preacher of the past. He was so well known that visitors would go out of their way to attend worship at his church so they could hear him preach. One Sunday he got sick just before it was time for the service to start. His brother was called upon to preach that morning. When it came time for the message several in the audience were disappointed that Henry Ward Beecher was not preaching. They got up to leave. At that point Beecher's brother announced, "All who came to worship Henry Ward Beecher may now leave. Those who came to worship Jesus Christ the Lord may remain seated."

Several years ago, the executives of Disney World were surprised to find from exit surveys they took that many families were leaving the theme park disappointed. Do you know why? They had come to see somebody but during their visit they had never crossed paths with him. His name was Mickey Mouse. So Disney executives created a way that everyone who wanted to see Mickey Mouse would be able to do that. Now at noon and as the park closes there is a parade down Main Street with you-know-who leading the way. The result was that now nearly everyone leaves the park happy because they got to see Mickey Mouse.

Every week the church has worship and the Lord's Supper is served so that everyone who wants to has the opportunity to see Jesus. Whatever reason you have for going to worship, I hope you leave having seen Jesus. That way no matter how well or poorly the preaching is, you have met the one who can meet your needs and save your soul.

Discussion Questions

1. Why wasn't it hard for the religious leaders to find Jesus?

2. What is the significance of being "at" worship?

3. How many adult men are required to have a Synagogue?

4. What attitude did the man with the withered hand have about worship?

5. What question should we always ask ourselves when we go to worship?

6. Who do you go to worship to see?

7. What could you do to make your worship more meaningful?

Chapter 8

"The Problem Of Popularity"
Mark 3:7-19

Jesus withdrew to the sea with His disciples; and a great multitude from Galilee followed; and also from Judea, ⁸ and from Jerusalem, and from Idumea, and beyond the Jordan, and the vicinity of Tyre and Sidon, a great number of people heard of all that He was doing and came to Him. ⁹ And He told His disciples that a boat should stand ready for Him because of the crowd, so that they would not crowd Him; ¹⁰ for He had healed many, with the result that all those who had afflictions pressed around Him in order to touch Him. ¹¹ Whenever the unclean spirits saw Him, they would fall down before Him and shout, "You are the Son of God!" ¹² And He earnestly warned them not to tell who He was. ¹³ And He went up on the mountain and summoned those whom He Himself wanted, and they came to Him. ¹⁴ And He appointed twelve, so that they would be with Him and that He could send them out to preach, ¹⁵ and to have authority to cast out the demons. ¹⁶ And He appointed the twelve: Simon (to whom He gave the name Peter), ¹⁷ and James, the son of Zebedee, and John the brother of James (to them He gave the name Boanerges, which means, "Sons of Thunder"); ¹⁸ and Andrew, and Philip, and Bartholomew, and Matthew, and Thomas, and James the son of Alphaeus, and Thaddaeus, and Simon the Zealot; [19] and Judas Iscariot, who betrayed Him.

INTRODUCTION

J. VERNON MCGEE TELLS OF a rose Bowl Parade he was watching just before World War II. He tells as he was watching the parade that the Standard Oil Company float came to a complete stop. It ran out of gas right in front of where he was viewing the parade. He says, "I couldn't help but laugh. If there was one float that should not have run out of gas, it was that one." McGee went on to say, "As I looked at that float, I saw a picture of many Christians today. They are beautiful, but they have no power in their lives."

Jesus was both God and man. Physically He was running out of gas. Mark tells us that Jesus withdrew to the sea (Sea of Galilee). He probably went back to Capernaum.

The Crush of the Crowd

Jesus withdrew because of the growing opposition He was facing from the religious leaders who were looking for a charge they could use to have Him arrested and because of His growing popularity among the people.

Jesus had preformed miracles and healed people. The word was getting around and crowds were growing. People were coming not only from Galilee, but from Jerusalem and Judea a hundred miles away and from Idumea, from beyond the Jordan and from Tyre and Sidon.

The number of people was so great that Jesus had the disciples keep a boat ready in case the crowd got out of control. Commentators suggest that there could have been as many as 10,000 people following Jesus. The crowd pressed against Jesus believing that if they could just touch Him they would be healed.

This scene reminds me of shoppers gathered outside a store on Black Friday waiting for the doors to open. In fact, the word "crowd" here can mean crush. Verse 9 of The Message Bible says, "He told his disciples to get a boat ready so he wouldn't be trampled by the crowd."

The crowd did not understand why Jesus came. He came to serve, preach the gospel (Mark 1:14, 15) and overthrow the power of evil. The demons knew who Jesus was. They even shouted it out. They said, "You are the Son of God!" The crowd followed Jesus for selfish reasons. They wanted healed. They wanted to see another miracle. They didn't really care who He was.

Jesus didn't come to be popular. He was not about to allow His popularity to keep Him from His mission of preaching the Gospel to save the lost and overcoming evil. Even though the crowds were coming for the wrong reasons Jesus healed them and cast out demons. He cares for the crowd, yet He withdrew from them and went up on the mountain.

The Calling of the Twelve

Moses got some good advice from his father-in-law when he was trying to judge Israel all by himself. Jethro encouraged Moses to put other men in charge of some of the disputes (Exodus 18). This lessened the burden on Moses so he didn't have to settle all the disputes.

Jesus withdrew and went up on the mountain taking twelve of His followers with Him whom He called and appointed to help Him in the work of preaching the gospel and casting out demons.

The word "called" (verse 13) is "summoned" in the NASV. It means to offer an urgent invitation to accept responsibilities for a certain task. Have you ever been summoned to serve on a jury? Jesus wanted these He called to be more than just a part of the crowd that followed Him. Verse 14 says that Jesus called these twelve "so that they would be with Him". The New Living Translation says "so they can be His regular companions".

Following Jesus, becoming a Christian, means that we want to spend time with Him and be His companion.

The twelve Jesus called were Simon Peter, James and John who were sons of Zebedee, Andrew, Philip, Bartholomew, Matthew, Thomas, James the son of Alphaeus, Thaddaeus, Simon the Zealot, and Judas Iscariot,

CONCLUSION

We have to be careful. Just because something is popular and everyone is doing it doesn't make it right. People came to Jesus for the wrong reasons. We can follow Jesus for the wrong reasons too.

Jesus said that wide is the way that leads to destruction and there are many people who are going down that popular road. Narrow is the road that leads to eternal life and few are traveling down that road.

Jesus is calling all of us to come be with Him and help Him spread the gospel and defeat the power of evil. Jesus will supply all the power you need. If you accept Jesus' summons and follow Him you will never run out of gas!

Discussion Questions

1. Why did Jesus withdraw to the Sea of Galilee?

2. How many people were probably following Jesus at this time?

3. Why were people following Jesus?

4. Why did Jesus have the disciples have the boat on standby?

5. What is the idea of the word "summoned?"

6. How many of the 12 disciples that Jesus took with Him can you name?

7. Why are you following Jesus?

Chapter 9

"Binding The Strong Man"
Mark 3:20-27

And He came home, and the crowd gathered again, to such an extent that they could not even eat a meal. [21] When His own people heard of this, they went out to take custody of Him; for they were saying, "He has lost His senses." [22] The scribes who came down from Jerusalem were saying, "He is possessed by Beelzebub," and "He casts out the demons by the ruler of the demons." [23] And He called them to Himself and began speaking to them in parables, "How can Satan cast out Satan? [24] If a kingdom is divided against itself, that kingdom cannot stand. [25] If a house is divided against itself, that house will not be able to stand. [26] If Satan has risen up against himself and is divided, he cannot stand, but he is finished! [27] But no one can enter the strong man's house and plunder his property unless he first binds the strong man, and then he will plunder his house.

INTRODUCTION

WHEN I THINK OF STRONG men I think of the strong man competitions on TV. I think of the incredible Hulk, Superman, Arnold Swartzeneger or Andre Roussimoff. At age 12 Andre was 6'3" and weighed 200 pounds. By the time he was an adult he was 7'4" and weighed 500 pounds. wrists were 12" around. You probably remember him as Andre the Giant of WWF fame. He could pick up a 250-pound man with one hand and throw him down like a doll. When I think of strong men in the Bible, I think of Samson who carried the gates of Gaza up a hill. He slew thousands of Philistines, yet he was robbed of his strength by Delilah.

Our text talks about "binding the strong man" so his house can be plundered (verse 27). There was a difference of opinion as to who the strong man was and how to bind him. Let's look at the strong man.

THE CROWD'S STRONG MAN

The crowd wanted to bind Jesus and make Him their king because they had seen his miraculous powers. They were looking for someone strong enough to overthrow the powerful Romans and deliver them. Look at some of the events Mark has given us so far:

Jesus taught as one having authority (1:22); He cast out the unclean spirit from the man in the Synagogue (1:23); Peter's mother-in-law was healed (1:30); Jesus healed all the sick and demon possessed in the city (1:34); Jesus preached to all the cities in Galilee and cast out demons (1:39); Jesus healed a leper (1:40); people were coming to Jesus from everywhere (1:45); the paralytic has his sins forgiven and he is healed (2:5, 12); Jesus heals the man with the withered hand (3:5); people were coming to Jesus from everywhere around (3:7,8); Jesus healed many (3:10); and unclean spirits fell down before Jesus (3:11).

Is it any wonder why the crowds wanted Jesus to be their king? They thought He was strong enough to restore the kingdom of Israel and overthrow the Roman oppression. He had the power!

HIS OWN FAMILIY'S STRONG MAN

Jesus' own relatives wanted to bind him because they thought He was crazy. He wasn't taking care of Himself. He wasn't getting enough rest or eating properly (verse 20).

When Jesus' family heard what was going on they made the two-day trip from Nazareth to Capernaum (verse 21). They were going to take custody of Him (verse 21). "Take custody of Him" means lay hands on him with force and restrain Him (like in a straight jacket).

Jesus was at the peak of His popularity but His own family thought He was crazy. They thought He had "lost His senses" - gone mad, became deranged, was out of His mind, and was crazy.

THE ENEMIES' STRONG MAN

Jesus' enemies wanted to prove that He was Satan. Jesus' enemies were the Scribes and Pharisees who were the religious leaders of the Jews. They didn't like it that the people were following Jesus instead of them. They had already begun plotting against Him by trying to find accusations so they could kill Him.

They claimed Jesus was possessed by Beelzebub - Satan. They said He cast out demons by the ruler of the demons (verses 22). Jesus' answer to this accusation was given in two parables: Verse 23 - How can Satan cast out Satan? and Verse 24 - a divided kingdom cannot stand.

The only way to steal from a strong man is to bind him first because he will defend himself if he isn't bound. Jesus could not be Satan because it would take someone stronger than Satan to bind Him.

CONCLUSION

The strong man is Jesus. Only Jesus can bind Satan and put him in his place. Only Jesus is strong enough to set the captives free Jesus has done that by going to the cross. Only Jesus Christ is strong enough to keep you from going to hell.

From Itasca, TX, comes this true story. is a memorial to 263 children who died when the local school caught on fire and was destroyed. Almost every family in the town was touched in some way by this tragedy. The school board vowed that this would never happen again and so when the new school was built they had a state of the art sprinkler system installed. Back then that was rare. When the school was built, Jr. High students were trained to give tours of the new school building. A big celebration and dedication ceremony was held along with a memorial service for the 263 students who died in the fire. People came from all over to see the new building and sprinkler system. It wasn't until several years later when a building expansion was needed that it was discovered that the state of the art sprinkler system had never been connected to any water supply. All those years, and not hooked up to the water supply.

Are you connected to Jesus Christ? He is the strong man who alone can take you to heaven.

Discussion Questions

1. How do most people try to stop a strong man?

2. Why did the crowd want to bind Jesus?

3. What were some of the things Jesus had done that made the people think He was strong?

4. Why did Jesus' own family want to take custody of Him?

5. Who did Jesus' enemies want to prove He was?

6. Why should we be connected to the strong man Jesus?

7. What can you do to stay connected to Jesus and why is that so important?

Chapter 10

"Behold, Your Mother and Your Brothers"
Mark 3:28-35

"Truly I say to you, all sins shall be forgiven the sons of men, and whatever blasphemies they utter; [29] *but whoever blasphemes against the Holy Spirit never has forgiveness, but is guilty of an eternal sin"* — [30] *because they were saying, "He has an unclean spirit."* [31] *Then His mother and His brothers *arrived, and standing outside they sent word to Him and called Him.* [32] *A crowd was sitting around Him, and they *said to Him, "Behold, Your mother and Your brothers are outside looking for You."* [33] *Answering them, He *said, "Who are My mother and My brothers?"* [34] *Looking about at those who were sitting around Him, He *said, "Behold, My mother and My brothers!* [35] *For whoever does the will of God, he is My brother and sister and mother."*

INTRODUCTION

REMEMBER THAT THE THEME FOR these studies is "To Serve with Love." Our theme verse is Mark 10:45 - "For even the Son of man did not come to be served, but to serve, and to give His life a ransom for many."

A recent Bible College graduate had just begun a new preaching ministry and was adjusting to preaching every Sunday. One area he was weak in was illustrations. He had heard an older minister tell a story that would fit well with the message he was working on. The story went like this: "The older minister told how he had spent some of the happiest moments of his life in the arms of another man's wife. That woman was my mother the minister said." Sunday came and the new minister started telling the illustration. "Some of the happiest moments of my life were spent in the arms of another man's wife". He paused in deep thought..."But for the life of me, I can't remember who she was."

We want to look at family. Look with me at Jesus' family. We will see that sometimes family is much more than flesh and blood.

In this text, Jesus' mother and brothers want him to stop ministering to people so they can talk to Him. Jesus wants us to meet His forever family.

Jesus' Earthly Family

Jesus had returned to Peter's home in Capernaum (3:20). We have already looked at the passage (Mark 3:20-27) where Jesus' family wanted to bind Him and take Him back to Nazareth because they thought He was crazy. They had made the 30-mile trip to take custody of Him when they found Him at Peter's house in Capernaum.

The mother of Jesus was Mary and His brothers were James, Joseph, Simon and Judas (Matthew 13:55, 56). We also know that Jesus had at least two sisters. John 7:5 adds that Jesus' brothers didn't believe in Him yet. When Jesus' family arrived at Peter's house in Capernaum, they fund such a crowd there because Jesus was teaching and performing miracles and they could not get in the door (Mark 3:31) so they send word in to Him.

When Jesus got the message, He used it as an opportunity to teach an important lesson about family. He asked, "Who are My mother and My brothers?"

Family that is Thicker than Flesh and Blood

Jesus answers His own question by gesturing with His hand and pointing to all those gathered around and sitting at His feet. He says, "Behold, My Mother and My brothers!" (verse 34). Jesus was not saying that our earthly family is not important. He was saying that there is more to family than flesh and blood. The more important family, are those who "do the will of God!" (verse 35).

There is a heavenly family that is more important than our earthly family. Our earthly family can be a part of our heavenly family but it seems that Jesus' earthly family had not yet understood who He really was.

What is the will of God that we are to do? Luke 8:21 puts it this way, "My mother and My brothers are those who hear the Word of God and do it." Simply put, God's will is for us to obey His Word.

James 4:17 says, "The one who knows the right thing to do, and does not do it, to him it is sin." Are we hearing God's Word and doing it?

One man seeking God's will closed his eyes, opened his Bible and let his finger fall on the page. He looked down and read, "Judas went out and hanged himself." He tried again and this time he read, "Go, thou and do likewise." Not satisfied he tried a third time. What he read said, "What you plan to do, do it quickly." I don't think that is what Jesus had in mind when He said, "Whoever does the will of God, he is My brother, and sister and mother" (Mark 3:35).

Joining God's Forever Family

When we study God's Word we begin to have faith and start trusting God. "Whoever believes in Him should not perish but have eternal life" (John 3:16). Our belief in Jesus causes us to realize that we have sinned and fallen short of the glory of God. This gives us the desire to change our heart and repent of our sin and start living for God (Luke 13:3 and Acts 2:38).

Once we change our hearts we want to tell others what Jesus means to us so we begin to confess Him with our mouth and by the way we live our lives (Matthew 10:32, 33).

The person who truly believes in Jesus is repentant and willingly confesses Christ, will want to be immersed into Him so that sins can be washed away and the gift of the Holy Spirit can come into their life (Acts 2:38 and Mark 16:16).

God's forever family is made up of those who have become a part of His family and are faithful to Him all of their life (Matthew 24:13, Rev. 2:10b, and Rev. 19:1-9).

CONCLUSION

The importance of family in Jewish society was so strong that Jesus' statement was radical. Jesus was saying that loving God was more important than loving mother or father or brothers and sisters (Matthew 10:37). be a part of God's family we have to hear God's Word and do His will. We really don't love Him unless we are doing His will and keeping His commandments (John 14:15).

An old-time preacher who didn't have much formal education was fond of saying, "Either you is or you ain't! What I mean by that is you are either saved or you are lost. You are either in God's family or you ain't. You are either a child of God or a child of the devil. You are either heaven bound or headed for hell. You have either been washed in the blood or you haven't been. I can't make a decision for you. Only you know if you is or you ain't a part of God's family."

Discussion Questions

1. Can you quote Mark 10:45? If not read it aloud.

2. In Matthew 13:55, 56 who is mentioned as being Jesus' family?

3. Who did Jesus say was His real forever family when he pointed to the crowd?

4. How do we join God's forever family?

5. Why was Jesus' statement that it was more important to love God than your parents so radical?

6. Where did this encounter take place?

7. In what way can you bless your forever family?

Chapter 11

"Making the WORD Produce"
Mark 4:1-9

He began to teach again by the sea. And such a very large crowd gathered to Him that He got into a boat in the sea and sat down; and the whole crowd was by the sea on the land. ² And He was teaching them many things in parables, and was saying to them in His teaching, ³ "Listen to this! Behold, the sower went out to sow; ⁴ as he was sowing, some seed fell beside the road, and the birds came and ate it up. ⁵ Other seed fell on the rocky ground where it did not have much soil; and immediately it sprang up because it had no depth of soil. ⁶ And after the sun had risen, it was scorched; and because it had no root, it withered away. ⁷ Other seed fell among the thorns, and the thorns came up and choked it, and it yielded no crop. ⁸ Other seeds fell into the good soil, and as they grew up and increased, they yielded a crop and produced thirty, sixty, and a hundredfold." ⁹ And He was saying, "He who has ears to hear, let him hear."

INTRODUCTION

EVERY YEAR, SEVERAL WEEKS BEFORE spring, I get seed catalogues in the mail. I like to look through them and plan my garden for the year. I usually don't order much from the catalogues but I get ideas for what to plant.

Here is something to think about: the seed of a globe turnip is only 1/20th of an inch big. Yet, when that seed is planted and cared for, it can increase its own weight 15 times every minute. With ideal growing conditions the globe turnip can increase its size 15,000 times. In a few months the turnip grows 27 million times larger than the seed it started from.

There are a few turnips we should plant. We need to "turnip" for Bible School and Church. We need to "turnip" for Bible Study in a small group. We need to "turnip" in support of our church and her mission. We need to "turnip" in serving the church and our community. Do you get my point?! This study is about the importance of producing. The emphasis Jesus makes here is how important it is to sew the seed. Let's look at the parable, its explanation and our hearts.

THE PARABLE

A sower goes out to sew some seed. Some of the seed falls

beside the road and is eaten by the birds (verse 4). Some seed falls on rocky ground and because there is no depth to the soil, the sun quickly withers the young sprouts and they die (verses 5,6). Some seed falls among thorns (weeds) and begin to grow but the tender plants are choked out so that they produce no crop (verse 7). Some seed falls on good ground and grows so well that these seeds produce a good yield, some 30, 60 or even 100 times more than what was planted (verse 8).

THE EXPLANATION

The great thing about this parable is that Jesus tells us what it means. He says the seed is the WORD of God. The sower is you and me. The soil is the hearts of people.

The seed that fell by the roadside and was eaten by the birds represents people who are on the go and too busy for the WORD of God. Satan comes along and takes the WORD away before it has a chance to start growing (verse 15).

The seed that fell on the rocky ground and withered under the heat of the sun because there was no depth to the soil is like people who gladly receive the WORD of God but they never let it take root in their lives. They have good intentions but afflictions, persecutions or other things cause them to fall away (verses 16, 17).

The seed that fell among the thorns represents those who hear the WORD of God but the worries of this world, deceitfulness of money and desires for other things choke out the WORD of God so that it is not fruitful (verses 18, 19).

The seed that was sown on the good soil represents those people who hear the WORD of God, accept it and let it produce 30, 60 or even 100 times in their lives.

THE KIND OF HEART

People's hearts must be prepared and ready for the WORD of God much like soil must be prepared for seed to be planted in it. This parable reveals four kinds of hearts. Which one do you have?

1. The HARD HEART. Satan uses many influences and activities of this world to harden our hearts to the WORD of God (Mark 4:4, 15).
2. The SHALLOW HEART. There is not much depth to a person's faith. It is like having a couple inches of soil on top of solid bedrock. This person is an emotional hearer who is ruled by the flesh and worldly desires. They buckle under pressure (Mark 4: 5, 6 and 16, 17).
3. The CROWDED HEART. There is no cultivating or weed control. The heart is divided. There is a struggle between good and evil, truth and falsehood. This is not a believing heart. You buy things you do not need to impress people you do not like with money you do not have (Mark 4:8, 20).
4. The FRUITFUL HEART. The WORD of God is heard, listened to, accepted, practiced, and obeyed. When the WORD of God gets in you and takes root, there is growth and a bountiful harvest that is 30, 60 or even 100 times what was planted. The amount of production varies according to our talents and abilities (Mark 4:8, 20).

CONCLUSION

You never know what the seeds you sow might produce.

Miss Thompson was a 4th grade teacher who had a student in her class that was listless, academically behind his classmates and generally non-responsive. Teddy had been passed each year without demonstrating the needed skills he should have. Miss Thompson grew weary of Teddy's apathy and one day spoke very harshly to him. She decided that Teddy just couldn't learn anything. One day Miss Thompson took time to read Teddy's file. Other teachers wrote, "Teddy needs academic help…no dad…his mom is sick…in need of professional counseling…Teddy's mom died…Teddy living with Aunt Mabel.

At Christmas each year the children would all bring a gift for their teacher. Teddy's gift was in a brown paper bag with tape holding the bag closed. She opened Teddy's gift. There was a half empty bottle of cheap perfume and an old bracelet. Miss Thompson was sensitive enough to put some of the perfume on and compliment Teddy in front of the whole class. Teddy stayed after school and said to Miss Thompson, "Miss Thompson, you smell just like my mother when she wore that perfume."

Miss Thompson cried all the way home and walked into her classroom the next day with a new mission - help Teddy no matter what. Teddy went on to graduate and attend college. Over the years he kept in contact with Miss Thompson. One day an invitation came in the mail to graduation exercises. In the invitation was a hand-written note. "Miss Thompson, I am graduating soon. I want you to sit in my mother's chair. You are the only family I really ever had." The note was signed, Theodore Salvard, MD.

Perhaps some seed you sow will produce beyond your expectations. We never know what the seeds we sow will accomplish. We never know what our serving our fellow man can do. We must sow the seed of God's WORD in other people's lives. He who sows sparingly will reap sparingly, but the person who sows bountifully will have an abundant harvest. How are you making the WORD produce?

Discussion Questions

1. Are you a good "turnip" for your church?

2. What do you think Jesus wanted us to see was important in this parable?

3. Can you name the four soils Jesus talked about in this parable?

4. What did Jesus say each of the soils represented?

5.   What are the four kinds of hearts that the four soils talk about?

6.   Do you know anyone like Teddy that you could help?

7.   What happens when we sow the Word of God in good soil?

Chapter 12

"The Kingdom of God"
Mark 4:26-32

And He was saying, "The kingdom of God is like a man who casts seed upon the soil; ^{27} *and he goes to bed at night and gets up by day, and the seed sprouts and grows — how, he himself does not know.* ^{28} *The soil produces crops by itself; first the blade, then the head, then the mature grain in the head.* ^{29} *But when the crop permits, he immediately puts in the sickle, because the harvest has come."* ^{30} *And He said, "How shall we picture the kingdom of God, or by what parable shall we present it?* ^{31} *It is like a mustard seed, which, when sown upon the soil, though it is smaller than all the seeds that are upon the soil,* ^{32} *yet when it is sown, it grows up and becomes larger than all the garden plants and forms large branches; so that* THE BIRDS OF THE AIR *can* NEST UNDER ITS SHADE.*"*

INTRODUCTION

WE HAVE LOOKED AT THE parable of the sower and saw that the emphasis there was on the importance of sowing the seed. In this lesson we will see that the emphasis is on the seed itself. We will look at the potential, the power and the progress of the seed.

The crowd wanted to make Jesus their king because they had witnessed His power and miracles. They thought He could overthrow the Romans and restore the kingdom they all had heard about. Since the kingdom was on the minds of the people, Jesus used the opportunity to teach them what the kingdom of God was like.

THE POTENTIAL OF THE SEED

We already know that the seed is the Word of God. "As small as a mustard seed" was a saying that commonly identified something as being small. Today we have sayings like "sharp as a tack" or "high as a kite" or "flat as a pancake" or "the check's in the mail." We know what is meant when we hear these sayings.

There is potential in every seed. When you plant seeds, you know what will grow from them. A small mustard seed can become a tree large enough for birds to build nests in.

Faith as small as a mustard seed can move mountains, Matthew 17:30 says. Within each of us there is potential. We can become the sons and daughters that God created us to become. It is sad and tragic when we don't reach our potential because of sin.

Just like seeds have genetic make ups, so do we. An apple seed will become an apple tree, a zucchini seed will become a zucchini plant. You and I were created to become the children of God.

God's Word will not return empty (Isaiah 55:11) and in Matthew 24:35 Jesus says, "Heaven and earth will pass away, but My words shall not pass away." When we sow God's Word it will produce because God has already put the potential in it.

THE POWER OF A SEED

We can't make a seed grow. We don't understand it. I can't explain it. It takes a great deal of faith and patience to be a farmer. The farmer plants the seed one day and goes to bed at night and after a few days when he wakes up the seed has sprouted (verse 27).

God puts the power to grow in seeds and in us. We can be seed growers and soil turners and we can water it but we can't make the seed grow. In 1 Cor. 3:6 Paul says, "I planted, Apollos watered, BUT God caused the seed to grow."

James 1:21 says we should "receive the implanted word which is able to save our soul." Romans 1:16 says. "For I am not ashamed of the Gospel (Word of God) for it is the power of God unto salvation to everyone who believes."

Look at Mark 4:27. It says that the seed sprouts up and grows - "how, he himself (farmer) does not know." Hebrews 4:12 says that the Word of God is sharper than any two-edged sword. We need to hope and trust in the power of the Word of God to do its job, to change people and to grow. All we can do is sow the seed!

THE PROGRESS OF THE SEED

Our job as Christians is to help promote the growth of the Word any way we can. We can prepare the soil, we can cultivate, we can water, fertilize, weed etc.

You don't plant seed one day and harvest it the next. All seeds have a growth period. From the time the seed is planted until the fruit is harvested there must be progress. Verse 28 says, "first the blade, then the head, then the mature grain in the head." It takes time. It sometimes is fast and sometimes slow but there is always progress. In us the progress may vary also, but there must always be progress or we will die.

Seed is sown knowing that there will be a harvest if everything goes as it should. We should sow expectantly. When the crop is ready, the farmer immediately puts the sickle to it so he gets the best possible harvest. Jesus began with 12 disciples. Soon there were 120 followers. On Pentecost (Acts 2) the number swelled by about 3,000. And then about 5,000 more men were added (Acts 4:4). Today, the church that Jesus established, that not even the gates of hell could destroy, has progressed into the millions.

The description of a mustard seed becoming a large tree that birds can build their nests in is a description of the kingdom of God! It may have started out a small seed but it has potential. Its power is released and it makes progress and becomes a tree. So it is with the church, the kingdom of God, when we sow the seed.

Galatians 6:9 says, "In due season we shall reap if we do not grow weary".

CONCLUSION

We are all laborers together with God. We should always remember though, that it is God who causes the growth. It is the Lord who adds those who are being saved to the church (kingdom) (Acts 2:47). It is the Lamb who writes our name down in the Lamb's book of life. Praise God we know that His kingdom will not fail. Not even hell can prevail against it. He has even promised to be with us to the end of the world. Our God has put within the seed we are to sow, the potential, the power and the progress. If we sow He will do the rest. If we are a part of the kingdom of God we will not be disappointed. A kingdom has a King. It has rules, and it has subjects who follow the King's commands. If you are not a part of the kingdom of God you can be. Would you trust and obey our Lord's commands? There is no other way whereby you can be saved.

Discussion Questions

1. Why do you think Jesus used a mustard seed to describe what the kingdom of God is like?

2. What kind of fruit does sowing the Word of God produce?

3. Where does the power for the seed to grow come from?

4. Whether it is a seed or us, what must always be happening?

5. Can you show how the seed of the Word of God produces over time?

6. What three things has God put in every seed we are to sow?

7. How are you doing at sowing the Word of God and what could you do to improve?

Chapter 13

"Even the Wind and Sea Obey Him"
Mark 4:35-41

On that day, when evening came, He said to them, "Let us go over to the other side." ³⁶ Leaving the crowd, they took Him along with them in the boat, just as He was; and other boats were with Him. ³⁷ And there arose a fierce gale of wind, and the waves were breaking over the boat so much that the boat was already filling up. ³⁸ Jesus Himself was in the stern, asleep on the cushion; and they woke Him and said to Him, "Teacher, do You not care that we are perishing?" ³⁹ And He got up and rebuked the wind and said to the sea, "Hush, be still." And the wind died down and it became perfectly calm. ⁴⁰ And He said to them, "Why are you afraid? Do you still have no faith?" ⁴¹ They became very much afraid and said to one another, "Who then is this, that even the wind and the sea obey Him?"

INTRODUCTION

THE PROOF'S IN THE PUDDING, the handwriting is on the wall. The check is in the mail. All the i's are dotted and the t's crossed. It's money in the bank. These are all statements that we use to emphasize sure things. In our text, Jesus is putting the disciples to the test to see if their faith is a sure thing.

He has already taught them the parable of the sower and the mustard seed in this chapter. Both of these parables were designed to teach them about faith. Now Jesus wanted to see if they had learned anything. It was around evening of the same day He had taught these parables (verse 35). Jesus was going to use a storm to test their faith.

STORMS WILL COME

We can't always control the storms of life but we can control how we face them when they come. This storm came up suddenly as they often do on the Sea of Galilee because of the terrain. The disciples didn't see it coming. It was an especially fierce storm that scared even the disciples who were fisherman on this sea.

Verse 37 says the wind was so strong that the waves were breaking over the sides of the boat and it was starting to fill up. The storms of life that we face come from three places: 1) outside sources, 2) our own sin, or 3) from the Lord.

Many people think that difficulty, storms and trials come into our lives because we have sinned. That may be true sometimes. But here the storm the disciples were going through happened even though they had obeyed the Lord by getting into the boat and heading for the other side of the Sea of Galilee.

Sometimes storms are necessary for our spiritual growth. Look at how Jesus referred to the disciples in verse 40 - "faithless." He was trying to teach them an important lesson.

We need to recognize that we are going to have storms come into our lives. How we react to and handle them when they come is important. Do we have enough faith to trust God? Do we really practice our faith or do we just talk about it?

STORMS SHOULD NOT BE FEARED

The disciples thought that Jesus was unaware of their problem. We often think that Jesus is unaware of our difficulties, too. But Jesus knows and cares all about us. He knows the number of hairs on our head (Matthew 10:30). 1 Peter 5:7 says that we can cast all of our cares upon Him because He cares for us.

There are 3 reasons why the disciples didn't need to fear the storm: 1)

Jesus promised they were going to the other side; 2) Jesus was with them in the boat; 3) Jesus was at peace sleeping during the storm.

Jesus was sleeping in the back of the boat so the disciples had to wake Him up. They ask a penetrating question in verse 38: "Don't you care that we are perishing?" Jesus rebuked the wind and the waves and said, "Hush, be still" (verse 39).

Immediately the wind died down and it became a fly fisherman's dream - perfectly calm. Talk about a real attention getter! The application here is that God will not allow us to have more difficultly and storm than we can handle. Storms are sure to come but we have a God who cares and goes through the storms of life with us. As long as Jesus is in your boat there is nothing to fear.

THE STORMS ARE NOT THE REAL PROBLEM

The disciples thought that the wind and the waves were the problem. The real problem wasn't the storm, but their lack of faith (verse 40). Jesus was showing the disciples and us that all power belongs to Him. Once Jesus got their attention after the calming of the storm, the disciples asked, "Who then is this, that the winds and the sea obey Him?"

When we go through storms in our lives we often look everywhere but where we should for help. One day a man fell into a pit and he couldn't get out. A subjective person came along and said, "I really feel for you down there." An objective person came along and said, "It is logical that someone would come along and fall down in there." A Christian Science member came along and said, "You only think you have fallen into a pit." A Pharisee said, "Only bad people fall into pits." A mathematician calculated how the man fell into the pit. A news reporter wanted an exclusive story of his pit. A fundamentalist said, "You deserve your pit." Confucius said, "If you would have listened to me, you would not have fallen into that pit." Buddha said, "Your pit is only a state of mind." A realist said, "Now that's a pretty nice pit." A scientist calculated the pressure necessary in pounds and inches to get the man out of the pit. A geologist told him to appreciate the rock strata in the pit walls. An evolutionist said, "You are a rejected mutant destined to be removed from the evolutionary cycle." In other words, the man is destined to die in the pit without producing any pit-falling offspring. The county inspector asked the man, "Do you have a permit for that pit?" A professor gave him a lecture on "The elementary principles of a pit." An evasive person came along and avoided the subject of the man's pit altogether. A self-pitying person said, "You haven't seen anything until you have seen my pit." The charismatic said, "Just confess that you are not really in a pit." The optimist said, "Things could be worse." The pessimist said, "Things will definitely get worse."

And then Jesus came along. He saw the man in the pit, stretched out his hand, and pulled the man out of the pit, set his feet on solid ground and helped him go on his way."

The application here is that we had better not get caught up in the storm or problem because the real problem is our lack of faith and trust in the Lord. He has promised never to forsake us but to be with us even to the end of the world (Matthew 28:20).

CONCLUSION

Christ and the disciples in a boat on a stormy sea were understood by the early church to be symbolic of the church existing in a troubled and sinful world. When we understand that Jesus is with us every moment of every day, we can make it through the storms that we encounter in our lives.

Jesus wanted the disciples and us to put our faith into action. He wanted us to be doers of the Word, not forgetful hearers (James 1:22). The disciples didn't yet get it that Jesus was the Son of God, the Messiah, and the One who would take away the sins of the world. If they realized who Jesus was, they never would have asked, "Who then is this, that even the wind and the sea obey Him?"

Have you come to realize who Jesus is?

Discussion Questions

1. What is the one sure thing in this lesson?

2. What did Jesus hope to find out by using this storm?

3. We may not be able to control the storms of life but what can we control?

4. What three places do the storms of life come from?

5. When we think Jesus doesn't care what's happening to us, what should we remember?

6. How did the wind and the waves stop?

7. What was the real problem in these verses?

Chapter 14

"Turn Your Heart Toward Home"
Mark 5:1-20

They came to the other side of the sea, into the country of the Gerasenes. ² When He got out of the boat, immediately a man from the tombs with an unclean spirit met Him, ³ and he had his dwelling among the tombs. And no one was able to bind him anymore, even with a chain; ⁴ because he had often been bound with shackles and chains, and the chains had been torn apart by him and the shackles broken in pieces, and no one was strong enough to subdue him. ⁵ Constantly, night and day, he was screaming among the tombs and in the mountains and gashing himself with stones. ⁶ Seeing Jesus from a distance, he ran up and bowed down before Him; ⁷ and shouting with a loud voice, he said, "What business do we have with each other, Jesus, Son of the Most High God? I implore You by God, do not torment me!" ⁸ For He had been saying to him, "Come out of the man, you unclean spirit!" ⁹ And He was asking him, "What is your name?" And he said to Him, "My name is Legion; for we are many." ¹⁰ And he began to implore Him earnestly not to send them out of the country. ¹¹ Now there was a large herd of swine feeding nearby on the mountain. ¹² The demons implored Him, saying, "Send us into the swine so that we may enter them." ¹³ Jesus gave them permission. And coming out, the unclean spirits entered the swine; and the herd rushed down the steep bank into the sea, about two thousand of them; and they were drowned in the sea. ¹⁴ Their herdsmen ran away and reported it in the city and in the country. And the people came to see what it was that had happened. ¹⁵ They came to Jesus and observed the man who had been demon-possessed sitting down, clothed and in his right mind, the very man who had had the "legion"; and they became frightened. ¹⁶ Those who had seen it described to them how it had happened to the demon-possessed man, and all about the swine. ¹⁷ And they began to implore Him to leave their region. ¹⁸ As He was getting into the boat, the man who had been demon-possessed was imploring Him that he might accompany Him. ¹⁹ And He did not let him, but He said to him, "Go home to your people and report to them what great things the Lord has done for you, and how He had mercy on you." ²⁰ And he went away and began to proclaim in Decapolis what great things Jesus had done for him; and everyone was amazed.

INTRODUCTION

I WAS JUST WONDERING? WHY ARE wrong phone numbers never busy? Do people in Australia call the rest of the world "up over?" Why is it called lipstick if you can still move your lips? Why is it that the night falls but the day breaks? Why is it that the third hand on your watch is called the second hand? Have you ever wondered how you get off a nonstop flight? Have you ever wondered why a dish called chili is so hot? Why do we call the time of day, when traffic is the slowest, rush hour? Why is lemonade made from artificial flavors and dish washing soap is made with real lemons? Why do we call it "Home Sweet Home" when we have never eaten it?

In this lesson we will look at a man who encountered Jesus and it changed him. In fact, he turned his heart toward home and the people marveled at his story. Let's let this man tell his own story.

THE TESTIMONY (verses 1-13)

I was a mad man because I had unclean spirits in me. These unclean spirits went by the name of Legion because they were many. A Legion in the Roman army has 6,000 soldiers. I lived in the tombs on the Northwest shore of the Sea of Galilee. Society had cast me out. Everyone was afraid of me and stayed away, and for good reason. The unclean spirits made me strong. I broke chains and no one could bind me. Day and night I cried out in pain and fear. Did I say I was a mad man? I even cut myself with sharp rocks.

My encounter with Jesus all started one evening when I saw a terrible storm out on the sea. And then, in an instant, everything was calm. Naturally, I went down to see what was going on. That is when I noticed a boat coming toward the shore. I learned later that the man in the boat had calmed the storm and saved those in the boat by telling the waves and the wind to be still.

As the boat came ashore I was about to let them have it when the unclean spirits controlling me recognized Jesus. So I fell down before Him. The unclean spirits called Him "The Son of the Most High God" and begged Him not to torment me. Jesus began to call out the unclean spirits in me. But the unclean spirits pleaded with Jesus not to send them out of the country. Instead they asked to be sent into a herd of pigs grazing nearby. Jesus permitted it. The pigs went crazy when the unclean spirits entered them. They ran down the bank and over the cliff falling into the sea where they drowned, about 2,000 of them.

I was feeling better already, just to be free of those unclean spirits. It had been a long time since I felt such freedom.

MY WITNESS (verses 14-17)

Those tending the pigs could not stop them from running off the cliff. They sure had a pig tale to tell! These men ran into the city to squeal to the pigs' owners about what had happened. They told everyone in the country and city about what they had witnessed.

It wasn't long before people were coming from everywhere to see what had happened. I don't think they believed the story they were told and they wanted to see for themselves. As they looked over the cliff they could seek pigs floating in the water! Pig floats anyone?! They also saw Jesus and me.

I was a changed man. I was no longer mad. I was calm and clothed. People seemed really surprised to see me in my right mind sitting at Jesus' feet. Those who had witnessed Jesus cast the unclean spirits out of me were now afraid of me because they feared Jesus who had healed me. The witnesses re-enacted the story just as they saw it happen. When the people heard the story again they were so afraid that they began asking Jesus to leave. I couldn't believe it! Jesus was right there with all that power to help them and change their lives for the better and they ask Him to leave? What a missed opportunity! I hope that if any of you ever see Jesus that you invite Him home with you. Sit at His feet and learn of Him. Don't turn Him away.

MY ACTIONS (verses 18-20)

Jesus was not going to stay where people didn't want Him. He got into the boat with the others and was preparing to leave. I really wanted to go with Him wherever He was going. It really didn't matter. Just to be near Him would be enough. But Jesus, who had cured me, said no! He said I couldn't go along. He told me I had to go home to my own people and tell them all about the great things He had done for me.

So, I did what He told me to do. I turned my heart toward home and began proclaiming all over Decapolis (the ten cities region where I grew up) which was on the East side of the Jordan River, South of the Sea of Galilee. Now I wasn't a preacher or anything. I had no training for what Jesus asked me to do. I just told people everywhere I went what Jesus did for me.

The people knew me and what I had been like. They marveled at the change Jesus had made in my life. It was as different as night and day. You know, you don't have to go off to a foreign country to be a missionary. Sometimes you can make a difference right in your own back yard. All you have to do is be willing to tell people what Jesus has done for you like I did.

CONCLUSION

One commentary suggested that the storm on the Sea of Galilee was caused by Satan because the devil didn't want Jesus to make it to the other side where the man with the unclean spirit was because he didn't want the man to become a witness for the Lord. That is a possibility. I do know that Satan does not like it when anyone makes a decision for the Lord.

A nurse in a pediatric ward would always let the children listen to their own heartbeat with her stethoscope before listening herself. The kids' eyes would always light up as they heard the thump, thump of their hearts. But she never got a response that equaled 4- year-old David's. As he listened intently to his own heartbeat, he got a grin on his face and said, "I can hear Jesus knocking!"

Have you let Jesus come into your heart? If not, you can today. Just obey His commands and surrender your will to Him. Jesus can change you just like He did the man with the unclean spirits.

Discussion Questions

1. What was the unclean spirit's name and how many of them could there have been?

2. What did the unclean spirits call Jesus?

3. How many pigs drowned?

4. What did the people who heard the story ask Jesus to do and why?

5. Jesus wouldn't let the man who was healed go with Him. What did He tell the man to do?

6. Who do you think caused the storm on the Sea of Galilee and why?

7. What testimony do you have that you can share with others?

Chapter 15

"No Laughing Matter!"
Mark 5:35-43

While He was still speaking, they came from the house of the synagogue official, saying, "Your daughter has died; why trouble the Teacher anymore?" 36 But Jesus, overhearing what was being spoken, said to the synagogue official, "Do not be afraid any longer, only believe." 37 And He allowed no one to accompany Him, except Peter and James and John the brother of James. 38 They came to the house of the synagogue official; and He saw a commotion, and people loudly weeping and wailing. 39 And entering in, He said to them, "Why make a commotion and weep? The child has not died, but is asleep." 40 They began laughing at Him. But putting them all out, He took along the child's father and mother and His own companions and entered the room where the child was. 41 Taking the child by the hand, He said to her, "Talitha kum!" (which translated means, "Little girl, I say to you, get up!"). 42 Immediately the girl got up and began to walk, for she was twelve years old. And immediately they were completely astounded. 43 And He gave them strict orders that no one should know about this, and He said that something should be given her to eat.

INTRODUCTION

LAUGHTER CAN BE A GOOD thing. Proverbs 17:22 is one of my favorite verses. The version I like best is, "Laughter is good medicine." Eccl. 3:4 says, "There is a time to weep and a time to laugh."

A man once counseled his son that if he wanted to live a long life he should sprinkle some gun powder on his cornflakes every morning. The son did this religiously and it worked. He lived to be 98. When he died he left 14 children, 28 grandchildren and 35 great grandchildren and a 15-foot hole in the side of the crematorium.

I heard Cotton Jones tell this story a few years ago. A man walked into a pet store and ordered 10 mice and 42 cockroaches. The pet store owner looked up and said, "That is a very unusual order." The customer replied, "Well, I'm moving out of my apartment and the lease agreement says that I must leave the apartment in the same condition I found it in or I don't get my deposit back."

Laughter can be healthy and therapeutic for you. People who laugh often live longer according to several medical studies. In our text verse 40, we find something that really is not a laughing matter.

The background of this text is that a man named Jairus, a Synagogue official, has come to Jesus desperate to have his 12-year-old daughter healed. She is very sick and Jairus has tried everything. Jairus was at the end of his rope but was willing to take a chance in going to Jesus for a healing for his daughter. The Jewish leaders were already out to get Jesus. At the very least he would make them mad or he could lose his job and his standing in the community. But Jairus had a great love for his daughter and he was willing to risk all to save her. He asks Jesus to go with him to his house to heal her. Jesus agrees to go.

On the way however, they are interrupted by a woman who has had a bleeding problem for twelve years. Jesus uses up precious time talking with the woman and healing her. After this interruption they continue on their journey to Jairus' house. But before they arrive they are met by messengers from Jairus' house bearing the bad news that the girl has died. They tell Jairus that there is no reason to bother Jesus any more. Let's look at the WORD Jesus has for these people.

A FAITHFUL WORD (verse 36)

Jesus said to Jairus, "Don't be afraid any longer, only *keep on believing.*" Jairus was faced with a choice. Would he believe his friends who said his daughter had died or would he believe Jesus who said she was just sleeping?

In our times of uncertainty, we have a choice to make also. Will we trust in the Lord? Will we listen to what our friends say? Will we be faithful to Him or will we depend upon our own strength?

Paul said, we may be afflicted in every way, but not crushed; perplexed but not despairing; persecuted, but not forsaken, struck down but not destroyed (2 Corinthians 4:8,9).

A HOPEFUL WORD (verse 39)

Jesus continued on to Jairus' home. When they arrived, they found a commotion of mourners weeping and crying loudly. A typical death in Palestine had burial the same day as the death with mourners hired to mourn loudly.

Everyone present at Jairus' house seemed to know that the girl had died but Jesus. He says the girl is not dead, she is just sleeping.

1. Thessalonians 4:13-16 says that the body sleeps until Jesus comes again and the resurrection takes place.
2. Corinthians 5:8 tells us that at death the spirit/soul of the Christian leaves the body and goes to be with the Lord.

Jesus was giving the people a hopeful word by telling them that she was just sleeping.

A LAUGHABLE WORD (verse 40)

When Jesus said Jairus' daughter was just sleeping, the people laughed at Him. They knew better.

In 1 Corinthians 1:18-21 we are told that the world sees Jesus and His message of the cross as foolishness. People have, are and will laugh at Jesus and Christians who follow Him. The world just doesn't believe His message and they don't accept Him.

But we need to remember that the power of the Lord is no laughing matter! Romans 1:16 says, "I am not ashamed of the Gospel, for it is the power of God unto salvation…"

The world looks at Jesus and Christians and sees fools chasing a hopeless end, but Christians see an endless hope in Jesus Christ.

A POWERFUL WORD (verse 41)

Jesus took Jairus, the girl's mother, Peter, James and John into the room where the girl was just "sleeping." According to Jewish law only two witnesses were necessary for verification purposes. Jesus takes five witnesses into the room but six come out!

Jesus speaks in Aramaic, "Talita kum," which means "little girl, I say to you, arise!" The power was in Jesus to speak a word and it would happen. "Immediately" the little girl got up and began walking. What do you think? Was she dead or just sleeping?

CONCLUSION

The crowd wasn't laughing now! Verse 42 says they were astonished! Jesus will increase our faith if we give Him the chance. He will be our hope. We need to take Jesus seriously because our eternal destination is at stake. Only Jesus Christ has the power to restore life.

Are we going to laugh at Jesus or are we going to take Him seriously? Are we living our lives thinking that the things of God are foolish? You can laugh at God now if you want to, but you won't be laughing when you have to stand before Him on judgment day.

There is a tradition that says the daughter of Jairus became a witness for the Lord the rest of her life. Her testimony won many to Christ. Jesus changed her. She could do no less than live her life for Him. She was dead, but Christ made her alive. He can do the same for you. If you know Jesus as your Savior, are you witnessing for Him? Can people see that the power of God has changed you?

Where do you plan on spending eternity - in the smoking or non- smoking section?

Your eternity is no laughing matter! Please take it seriously.

Discussion Questions

1. Who was Jairus and why was he so desperate?

2. What interruption happened as Jesus was on the way to Jairus' house?

3. What faithful word did Jesus give Jairus that forced Jairus to make a choice?

4. What was the response when Jesus told the mourners that the girl was just sleeping?

5. When we put our hope and trust in the Lord, what does the world think of us?

6. How many witnesses went into where the girl was "sleeping?"

7. What does tradition tells us about Jairus' daughter?

Chapter 16

"Shake Those Dirty Feet"
Mark 6:7-13

And He summoned the twelve and began to send them out in pairs, and gave them authority over the unclean spirits; [8] *and He instructed them that they should take nothing for their journey, except a mere staff — bread, no bag, no money in their belt —* [9] *but to wear sandals; and He added, "Do not put on two tunics."* [10] *And He said to them, "Wherever you enter a house, stay there until you leave town.* [11] *Any place that does not receive you or listen to you, as you go out from there, shake the dust off the soles of your feet for a testimony against them."* [12] *They went out and preached that men should repent.* [13] *And they were casting out many demons and were anointing with oil many sick people and healing them.*

INTRODUCTION

THERE WAS A GREAT LOSS in the entertainment world recently. Larry LaPrise from Detroit, MI, passed away. He was 83. His death was especially difficult for Larry's family. They had a hard time keeping Larry in his casket. You see, Larry was the author of the song, "The Hokey Pokey." The family would put Larry's right foot in…and well, you know the rest of the story!

Today, we are looking at shaking feet, but not that kind. I am talking about the kind that Jesus told the twelve disciples about. The Twelve had spent a lot of time with Jesus by now, listening to His teaching and seeing Him perform miracles. Jesus knew they had learned a lot but He also knew that the best way they would learn was with a trial run.

Like a wedding rehearsal, your first pancake, practicing putting, a walkthrough of a house, a sermon, trying on a new dress, or test driving a new car, you want to check things out first. Jesus "summoned the Twelve and began to send them out in pairs" (verse 7). It was time for an "internship" to give the Twelve a real firsthand learning experience.

After the death, burial and resurrection of Jesus, the church would be established and the Twelve would begin their own ministries. Verse 12 says that they went out and preached. It is every Christian's responsibility to go out and tell others about Jesus.

Where Jesus ministered there are two seas. One sea is alive with fish and it is surrounded by vegetation and trees. The other sea is dead and has very little life in it. There are no plants or trees. The first sea is the Sea of Galilee. It takes in water from the north and gives it off to the south. The water it gives off is the Jordon River. This fresh water travels about 90 miles and empties into the second sea called the Dead Sea. The reason it is dead is because it doesn't give up its water. It keeps it and it becomes salty and almost everything around it dies.

The same thing can happen to us if we don't share our faith. You and I need to share our faith. As a church we can't keep the Good News to ourselves. We must share it or the same thing can happen to us that happened to the fresh water of the Jordon when it gets to the Dead Sea.

Jesus knew that if the Twelve could experience the joy of sharing the Gospel, they would be forever changed. There is no greater feeling than helping win someone to Christ. This text tells us that we must share our faith. We must go with authority, urgency and trust.

We Must Go with Authority

"Summoned" (verse 7) means to call or invite. Who among us would refuse Jesus' invitation? Yet, that is what we do when we do not go.

"In pairs" (verse 7) means duo, duo. A legal witness was two. When there were two, one could encourage and pray for the other. They could also learn from each other (Ecclesiastes 4:9-12).

"Send them out" (verse 7) refers to "an apostle or an ambassador" who is sent out on behalf of another. The one sent is as the one who does the sending.

"Authority" (verse 7) means this band of ordinary men represented an extraordinary God. 2 Corinthians 3:5-6 says that our adequacy comes from God.

What God enables, He also empowers. When God calls people to a job, He also gives them the authority and power to complete it.

We Must Go with Urgency

No excess baggage (verse 8) was to be taken. Nothing should slow us down or tie us down by keeping us from doing the task we were sent to do.

Having a lot of stuff tends to take time to manage and care for. We can't afford to waste time or effort. We get the idea that there was a sense of urgency about what the Lord wanted done.

Hospitality and hostility can be expected. Both good and bad things will be encountered as we go. The parables of the drag net and tares make that clear.

"Shake off the dust from the soles of your feet" (verse 11) was a Jewish custom. It showed an act of cleansing Gentile dust from off their feet. They would often do this as they came back into Jewish territory. It was an object lesson. It was a warning for not accepting the message and the messenger sent by God. If the Twelve and their message of repentance was rejected, it was the same as rejecting Christ Himself.

We Must Go with Trust

They were to take very little with them (verses 8, 9) because the Lord wanted them to learn to live by faith. Minimum provisions required the Twelve to depend upon God and taught them to have a maximum faith. We must take our message to people and depend on God to supply our needs.

Demons were cast out and sick were healed (verse 13). We must remember that this world is not our home. We are just passing through. "Wouldn't take nothing for my journey now, gotta make it to heaven somehow."

CONCLUSION

Are we willing to go for God? A faithful follower lives dependent upon the Lord. He or she travels light. They do not seek their own comfort first but they seek God's pleasure. They do not hesitate to tell people they need to repent of sin. If people will not listen, they go on and talk to others about Jesus.

If you are a Christian, then the Lord has given you authority, a sense of urgency and a faith that trusts God to go where He sends you each day. Are you going? Then you may have to shake those dirty feet!

Discussion Questions

1. Why was Jesus sending out the twelve on internships?

2. What can we learn from the Sea of Galilee and the Dead Sea?

3. What authority do we have when we go for the Lord?

4. What shows us that there is a sense of urgency about sharing the gospel?

5. Why did Jesus send the twelve out with minimal supplies?

6. What is the benefit of going out in pairs to talk to people about Jesus?

7. Who could you go and talk to about Jesus?

Chapter 17

"The Miracle Meal"
Mark 6:30-44

[43] and they picked up twelve full baskets of the broken pieces, and also of the fish. [44] There were five thousand men who ate the loaves. *The apostles gathered together with Jesus; and they reported to Him all that they had done and taught.* [31] *And He said to them, "Come away by yourselves to a secluded place and rest a while." (For there were many people coming and going, and they did not even have time to eat.)* [32] *They went away in the boat to a secluded place by themselves.* [33] *The people saw them going, and many recognized them and ran there together on foot from all the cities, and got there ahead of them.* [34] *When Jesus went ashore, He saw a large crowd, and He felt compassion for them because they were like sheep without a shepherd; and He began to teach them many things.* [35] *When it was already quite late, His disciples came to Him and said, "This place is desolate and it is already quite late;* [36] *send them away so that they may go into the surrounding countryside and villages and buy themselves something to eat."* [37] *But He answered them, "You give them something to eat!" And they said to Him, "Shall we go and spend two hundred denarii on bread and give them something to eat?"* [38] *And He said to them, "How many loaves do you have? Go look!" And when they found out, they *said,*

"Five, and two fish." ³⁹ And He commanded them all to sit down by groups on the green grass. ⁴⁰ They sat down in groups of hundreds and of fifties. ⁴¹ And He took the five loaves and the two fish, and looking up toward heaven, He blessed the food and broke the loaves and He kept giving them to the disciples to set before them; and He divided up the two fish among them all. ⁴² They all ate and were satisfied,

INTRODUCTION

THE FEEDING OF THE 5,000 is an amazing story of Jesus' miraculous power. It is so amazing, in fact, that it is one of the few events in Jesus' ministry that all four Gospel writers write about. But it is a little misleading. You see, verse 44 says that there were 5,000 men who ate. Now that is misleading because there were also women and children present. Culturally, women and children were generally not counted when numbers were given. We know children were present because Andrew found a boy who had 5 small loaves and two dried fish for his lunch (John 6:8, 9). In Matthew's account of this miracle meal he tells us that there were 5,000 men besides women and children (Matthew 14:21).

R.C. Foster, in his Studies on the Life of Christ, says that there could have been as many women and children present as there were men. So, we are really talking about feeding 10,000, not just 5,000. Whatever the number, we are awed by the magnitude of this miracle and the number of people that were fed by 5 loaves and 2 fish. And if that wasn't enough to blow our minds, verse 43 says that they picked up 12 full baskets of the leftovers.

This is definitely a miracle that would grab and hold your attention! Let's look at this miracle meal a little closer.

TOO BUSY TO EAT

The crowd of people presented a real opportunity for ministry that needed to be taken advantage of by the disciples. The crowd was coming and going. Jesus and the disciples were so busy that verse 31 says that they didn't even have time to eat.

Jesus was still teaching the disciples using the "learn as you go" method. Jesus and the disciples had just got the news that John the Baptist had been beheaded. They wanted to get away from the crowd to a solitary place to mourn John's loss. They got in a boat and put out on the Sea of Galilee for that solitary place. But the people could see them and ran around the lake after them.

When you are too busy to take time to eat you are too busy. We all need times of refreshing, retreat, and recharging. Jesus is our example here.

Vance Havner said, "If you don't come apart and rest, you will come apart."

Several men were in a boat on a dangerous river. One of the men who didn't know how to swim fell overboard and was drowning. One of the other men was a former Navy Seal. He reached down to grab the man by his arm. When he went to pull the man back into the boat his prosthetic arm came off and he went back under water. The former seal knew the man would come back up so he waited and this time he grabbed the man by his hair. But the man had a toupee so when he tried to pull the man into the boat it came off and the man went under again. The third time the seal grabbed the man by the leg, and you guessed it! He had a prosthetic leg. The next time the man surfaced the seal grabbed him by his pants and was finally able to pull him back into the boat. The saved man was spitting and sputtering as the seal said, "If you would have just held together I could have saved you sooner."

TOO PROUD TO SEE

The disciples saw the crowd and saw a problem rather than an opportunity. Jesus saw the crowd of people and had compassion for them. He saw sheep without a shepherd.

Jesus met the need of the people by teaching them and feeding them. When the people were hungry, the disciples' solution was to send them away so they could come up with food on their own or take up a collection to buy the bread they would need to feed everyone.

The disciples had not yet learned to see people through Jesus' eyes. Whenever we have a problem we need to look for the potential and the lessons the problem has for us.

How many things have been invented because of a problem? Helen Keller learned to sign even though she was deaf and blind because Ann Sullivan saw the potential rather than the problem. What do you see?

TOO TIGHT TO GIVE

Often we measure our resources and decide if we can give or do something based upon the results we get. Instead, we need to look for God's will and trust Him to meet the need.

Andrew (John 6:8, 9) found a boy who had a sack lunch of five loaves and two fish. Jesus took the loaves and fish, prayed to God, blessed and broke them into pieces and gave them to the disciples to pass out to the people. The "learn as you go" method was put into action.

When everyone had eaten and was "satisfied" (verse 42), Jesus had the disciples collect the leftovers which amounted to 12 full baskets. That is even more than they had when they started. Do you think the disciples learned something? The Lord can take what we are willing to give and multiply it so that there is more left over than when we began.

CONCLUSION

People want the gift but not always the giver. They want the privileges but not the responsibilities.

This miracle happened in Jesus' hands. We are not manufactures of miracles. We are just distributors like the disciples. 5 loaves and 2 fish fed 5,000 men plus women and children. And there was more left over than when they started. What a lesson for us. Jesus can take our little and make it much.

There are four things you can do with your hands: you can wring them in despair; you can fold them in idleness; you can clench them into fists in anger or you can use them to help someone. – (from *Bits and Pieces*, January 5, 1995, page 24).

What could Jesus do with you if you would put yourself in His hands? What could you do to help people if you saw them through Jesus' eyes?

Discussion Questions

1. What do you think is the number of people who were fed in this lesson?

2. What was used to feed these people?

3. How much was left over after everyone was satisfied?

4. What method was Jesus using to teach the disciples?

5. How should we learn to see people?

6. What can you do with your hands?

7. What lesson will you take away from this study?

Chapter 18

A Walk on the Wild Side
Mark 6:45-52

Immediately Jesus made His disciples get into the boat and go ahead of Him to the other side to Bethsaida, while He Himself was sending the crowd away. ⁴⁶ After bidding them farewell, He left for the mountain to pray. ⁴⁷ When it was evening, the boat was in the middle of the sea, and He was alone on the land. ⁴⁸ Seeing them straining at the oars, for the wind was against them, at about the fourth watch of the night He came to them, walking on the sea; and He intended to pass by them. ⁴⁹ But when they saw Him walking on the sea, they supposed that it was a ghost, and cried out; ⁵⁰ for they all saw Him and were terrified. But immediately He spoke with them and said to them, "Take courage; it is I, do not be afraid." ⁵¹ Then He got into the boat with them, and the wind stopped; and they were utterly astonished, ⁵² for they had not gained any insight from the incident of the loaves, but their hearts were hardened.

INTRODUCTION

KARL WALENDA, AT AGE 65, took a wild walk of 821 feet in 1970. He took 616 steps, but he was 750 feet above the Tallulah Gorge in

Georgia and he was walking on a cable a little less than 2 inches wide! The whole wild walk took about 20 minutes and Walenda stopped twice to do a headstand.

Walenda's walk was considered the highest tightrope walk until a few years ago when a 25-year-old Frenchman, Philippe Petit, nearly doubled the record with his 1350 feet above-ground walk between the Twin Towers of the World Trade Center in New York.

In this message, I want to tell you about a walk on the wild side that was even better than that. It was Jesus walking on the water in Mark 6: 45-52. The disciples had just experienced the feeding of the 5,000 and were riding a high from that experience. Jesus used this walk on the wild side to see if the disciples had learned anything from feeding the 5,000.

The people were so taken by Jesus' power to feed them that, according to John 6:14, 15, they were planning to take Jesus by force and make Him their king. Jesus sent the disciples away in a boat to Bethsaida, on the other side of the Sea of Galilee while He sent the multitude away (verse 45). He knew the disciples still had much to learn about faith.

Let's look at what Jesus' walk on the wild side can teach us.

JESUS KNOWS IT IS IMPORTANT TO PRAY

When life gets hectic and wild, we need to take time to pray. Jesus said farewell to the crowd and then went alone up the mountain to pray (verse 46). Jesus is praying on the mountain while the disciples are making their way to other side of the Sea of Galilee against a stiff wind.

It was the fourth watch of the night, 3-6am, and Jesus could see from where He was praying that the disciples were having trouble. They had left in the boat about dark so they had been rowing for some time. What do you suppose Jesus prayed about all this time? I am sure a big part of His praying was for the disciples. He was counting on them to carry on the work He started once He ascended back to the Father.

JESUS KNOWS WHAT IS HAPPENING IN OUR LIVES

There was a Passover full moon which allowed Jesus to see the disciples out in the middle of the Sea of Galilee from the mountain where He was praying. Jesus saw them straining at the oars because the wind was against them (verse 48).

The lessons learned from feeding the 5,000 were not on the disciples' minds as they were helpless and afraid in the midst of the storm. Their best effort was not enough. It was as if they took two steps forward and then one back.

The storms of life have a way of keeping us from moving forward. Jesus is just waiting for us to ask Him for help.

JESUS KNOWS HOW TO CALM OUR STORMS

Jesus came to the disciples walking on the sea (verse 48). Jesus acted as if He intended to pass on by. It seems He wanted the disciples to see Him, recognize who He was, trust Him and invite Him into the boat.

But the disciples didn't recognize Him. Instead they thought they were seeing a ghost (verse 49). This is the second storm the disciples have gone through. They went through another storm in Mark 4:35-41. Jesus was with the disciples asleep in the boat during the first storm. During this second storm Jesus is on the mountain praying for them. He was hoping they had learned to live by faith.

When the disciples didn't recognize Him he spoke, "Take courage; it is I, do not be afraid" (verse 50). Jesus got into the boat and immediately the wind stopped and the disciples were astonished (verse 51).

CONCLUSION

Jesus must have been very sad because verse 52 says that the disciples had not gained any insight from the feeding of the 5,000. In other words, they had not learned the lesson about faith and hope that Jesus was teaching them. Instead their hearts became hardened. Hard hearts come from failing to respond to truth and the lessons that are being taught. In Matthew 14:22-32, he tells us that Peter tried to walk on the water but began to sink so Jesus had to reach out and save him.

Dr. Wilbur Chapman had what he called "My rule for Christian living." "The rule that governs my life is this: anything that dims my vision of Christ, or takes away my taste for Bible study or cramps my prayer life or makes Christian work difficult is wrong for me, and I must turn away from it."

This simple rule may help you find a safe road for your feet as you walk on the wild side with Jesus. Are we learning from Jesus or are our hearts growing hard?

Discussion Questions

1. What were the people planning to do with Jesus because of His miraculous power?

2. Why did Jesus send the disciples on ahead to the other side of the Sea of Galilee?

3. The storms of life keep us from doing what?

4. What did Jesus say to the disciples when they thought they were seeing a ghost?

5. Did the disciples learn a lesson from the feeding of the 5,000? How do we know?

6. What happens when we don't learn faith lessons?

7. Do you agree with Dr. Wilbur Chapman's rule for Christian living?

Chapter 19

"The Heart of the Matter"
Mark 7:14-23

After He called the crowd to Him again, He began saying to them, "Listen to Me, all of you, and understand: ¹⁵ there is nothing outside the man which can defile him if it goes into him; but the things which proceed out of the man are what defile the man. ¹⁶ [If anyone has ears to hear, let him hear."] ¹⁷ When he had left the crowd and entered the house, His disciples questioned Him about the parable. ¹⁸ And He said to them, "Are you so lacking in understanding also? Do you not understand that whatever goes into the man from outside cannot defile him, ¹⁹ because it does not go into his heart, but into his stomach, and is eliminated?" (Thus He declared all foods clean.) ²⁰ And He was saying, "That which proceeds out of the man, that is what defiles the man. ²¹ For from within, out of the heart of men, proceed the evil thoughts, fornications, thefts, murders, adulteries, ²² deeds of coveting and wickedness, as well as deceit, sensuality, envy, slander, pride and foolishness. ²³ All these evil things proceed from within and defile the man."

INTRODUCTION

OUR HEART IS A HARD-WORKING marvel. It beats an average of 75 times a minute, 40 million times a year, two and a half billion times in the life of a 70-year-old. At every beat, the average heart disperses 4 ounces of blood. That amounts to 3,000 gallons a day or 650,000 gallons a year. That is enough blood to fill 81 tanker train cars that hold 8,000 gallons each. The heart produces enough energy in 70 years to lift the largest battleship completely out of the water.

In this study we want to see that the heart of the matter is the matter of the heart. That is really what is important. We want to keep the main thing the main thing.

EXTERNAL TRADITIONS ARE TRIVIAL

The Pharisees and Scribes were the religious leaders who made sure the ceremonial laws were followed. They were concerned because Jesus' disciples were not observing these man-made laws. If you wanted to be looked upon as religious, Jewish tradition demanded that you follow the man-made rules.

The heart of the matter was that the disciples of Jesus were eating without washing their hands (Mark 7:5). The Jewish leaders basically were saying, "You are what you eat!" That is a catchy saying but it is not true.

Jesus' response was, "There is nothing outside of the man which going into him can defile him; but the things which come out of the man are what defile the man" (verse 15). What you see is not always what you get. You can't judge a book by its cover.

INTERNAL REALITIES ARE REAL

Food goes into the stomach and then is eliminated. It is not what we put into our bodies that defile us. What defiles us is what comes out of our hearts.

Jesus said in verses 20-23, "That which proceeds out of the man, that is what defiles the man. [21] For from within, out of the heart of men, proceed the evil thoughts, fornications, thefts, murders, adulteries, [22] deeds of coveting *and* wickedness, *as well as* deceit, sensuality, envy, slander, pride *and* foolishness. [23] All these evil things proceed from within and defile the man."

If you want to know what a person is really like take a look at their attitudes, their character and their thoughts. This is the inside story!

Have you heard of "GIGO" - garbage in, garbage out? Here is a fundamental principal you can build your life upon: good comes out of us because we put good stuff in. What really matters is who we are on the inside, not what we appear to be on the outside. "You can fool some of the people all the time, and you can fool all the people some of the time, but you can't fool God any of the time!"

EXTERNAL CERTAINTIES ARE TO BE CULTIVATED

Maybe you have heard this catchy saying. "Only one life, 'twill soon be past; only what's done for Christ will last!" Eternity is a certainty. We must prepare our soul for the eternity we want.

There can be no pretending to follow Christ. We must be the real deal, the genuine article, not a counterfeit or a hypocrite. We must nourish the inner man by feeding our spirit with the Word of God and the things of God.

An apple a day may keep the doctor away but an onion a day keeps everyone away! What are you feeding your inner self? Good or bad things? Take a look at what is coming out of you or better yet, ask a trusted friend what they see coming out of you.

CONCLUSION

It all boils down to, what is our relationship with Jesus Christ? Unless we have an ongoing personal relationship with Him that we are feeding each day, it will be easy for the devil to defeat us. The good news is that we can change.

The Bible says that when we meet Christ in the water of baptism we clothe ourselves with Christ (Galatians 3:27). We need to take every thought captive to the obedience of Christ (2 Corinthians 10:5). We need to spend time letting our minds dwell on things above (Philippians 4:8). It is as simple as remembering to keep your eyes on Jesus and the wonder of His grace.

Helen H. Lemmel wrote these words in a song - "Turn your eyes upon Jesus, look full in His wonderful face, and the things of earth will look strangely dim in the light of His glory and grace."

The American Heart Association reports that 58,800,000 people suffer from some kind of cardiovascular disease in America. Coronary heart disease is the leading cause of death in the USA. Every 29 seconds someone in

America will suffer some kind of coronary event. Every minute someone in the US dies from heart disease.

But it is not just physical heart disease that we suffer from. Even worse is the spiritual heart disease that comes from people being far away from God. "Draw near to God and He will draw near to you" (James 4:8). "As a man thinks in his heart, so is he" (Proverbs 23:7).

In 1983 Dr. Wm. DeVries implanted the first permanent artificial heart in a human. After receiving permission for the experimental transplant, he had to choose one person from a list of 78 people who were desperately ill and saw the artificial heart as their only hope. Barney Clark, a retired 62-year-old dentist was selected and received the first artificial heart. He lived 112 days after the surgery. In 1984 Dr. DeVries was given permission to perform surgery on six more patients. He had to pick six people from a totally new list because the 77 left after Barney Clark was chosen had all died in the year that had passed.

Only the Lord can create a new and pure heart within us. How is your heart today? Does it belong to the Lord? That is really the heart of the matter.

Discussion Questions

1. What is the heart of the matter?

2. What did the religious leaders think was the heart of the matter that made you religious?

3. What is it that defiles a person?

4. What does "GIGO" mean?

5. What is a good way to check what is coming out of us?

6. What does the heart of the matter all boil down to?

7. Is your heart pumping for the Lord?

Chapter 20

"Some Crumbs for the Dogs"
Mark 7:24-30

Jesus got up and went away from there to the region of Tyre. And when He had entered a house, He wanted no one to know of it; yet He could not escape notice. ²⁵ But after hearing of Him, a woman whose little daughter had an unclean spirit immediately came and fell at His feet. ²⁶ Now the woman was a Gentile, of the Syrophoenician race. And she kept asking Him to cast the demon out of her daughter. ²⁷ And He was saying to her, "Let the children be satisfied first, for it is not good to take the children's bread and throw it to the dogs." ²⁸ But she answered and said to Him, "Yes, Lord, but even the dogs under the table feed on the children's crumbs." ²⁹ And He said to her, "Because of this answer go; the demon has gone out of your daughter." ³⁰ And going back to her home, she found the child lying on the bed, the demon having left.

INTRODUCTION

AN ELDERLY WOMAN WHO WAS well known for her faith would stand on her front porch and shout "Praise the Lord!" Next door to her lived an atheist who got angry every time she shouted "Praise the Lord!" He would shout back, "There ain't no Lord!" Hard times set in on the elderly lady and she began praying on the porch loud enough that the neighbor could hear her. Her prayer was simple. It went like this: "Lord, I need your help. Please send me some groceries." The next morning the woman went out on her front porch to pray and found several sacks of groceries. Loudly she shouted "Praise the Lord!" At that point the neighbor jumped out from behind the bushes and said, "Ha, ha, I told you there was no Lord. I bought these groceries and put them there. God had nothing to do with it." The lady started jumping up and down and clapped her hands. She prayed, "Praise the Lord! He not only answered my prayer of faith for groceries but He even made the Devil pay for them."

Planning for the future is important. We can't dwell on the past but hopefully the past can be a foundation for the future. Jesus would say after His resurrection just before He ascended into heaven, "You shall be My witnesses both in Jerusalem, and in all Judea and Samaria, even to the remotest part of the earth" (Acts 1:8).

In Mark 7:24-30, Jesus was preparing the disciples for the future. He is traveling to the area of Tyre and Sidon (40 miles west of Capernaum). This was Gentile country. Jesus had two reasons for going there: 1) He wanted to get away from the crowds and find a little peace and quiet. 2) He was trying to teach the disciples that the Gospel was for everyone, both Jews and Gentiles. Everyone should have the chance to enter the kingdom of God. There isn't one sinner that God doesn't love enough to send His only Son to save. This is a story about great faith.

AGAINST ALL ODDS

This woman was a Gentile, a Syrophenician or Canaanite. She had a daughter who was demon possessed. Jesus was a Jew, yet she came to Him and bowed down at His feet. She was a woman and Jesus was a man. This reminds us of the encounter Jesus already had with the woman at the well.

Satan was against her. Her daughter was demon possessed. The disciples were against her and wanted to send her away. For a brief moment it even appeared that Jesus was against her. She had to keep asking Jesus to heal her daughter (Mark 7:26). In Matthew's account of this (15:23) it says that Jesus did not answer a word.

The woman was persistent and didn't let any barrier keep her from appealing to Jesus for help for her daughter.

AGAINST ALL ETIQUETTE

In verse 27, Jesus finally responds to the woman's repeated cries for help. "The children" represents the Jews. "The dogs" represent the Gentiles.

The custom was that bread was used like a napkin. Since you ate with your fingers you wiped them off on the bread. Then you could eat the bread or throw it away. The woman's reply in verse 28 was, "Even the dogs eat the crumbs that fall from the children's table."

Jesus does not use the Greek word for dog here that was traditionally used by Jews to refer to Gentiles. That word would mean "dirty scavenger dogs." Instead, Jesus uses the word that means "little pet puppy lap dog."

FOR A GREAT FAITH

Jesus must have been pleased that the woman used His own words in her answer to Him, "even the dogs under the table feed on the children's crumbs" (verse 28).

It is very interesting that the only two times Jesus refers to people's faith being "great" is here with the Syrophenician woman and the Roman Centurion who sought healing for his servant (Matthew 8:5-13). Both of these were Gentiles.

Great faith is faith that takes God at His Word. In both these cases of "great faith", the healings happened instantly from a distance. This woman recognized Jesus, came to Him, and called Him "Son of David" and "Lord" (Matthew 15:22, 24, 27). She cried out for mercy (undeserved favor) at Jesus' feet.

The disciples wanted to send her away. But Jesus rewarded her for her great faith and persistence by healing her daughter at once.

When the woman got to her home she found her daughter in bed free from the demon that had once possessed her (Mark 7:30).

CONCLUSION

Great faith doesn't give up. Great faith takes God at His Word. Jesus went to Tyre and Sidon, verse 24 says, to escape notice; but He could not escape this persistent woman's notice.

God will not hide from us. In fact, He wants us to find Him. He shows Himself to us in His creation, in friendship, and in faith.

Our prayer should always be, "Lord, increase our faith!" Today you can know against all odds and against all etiquette that the Lord is for you and wants you to have a great faith.

Discussion Questions

1. What did Jesus prepare the disciples for in the future?

2. This study is a story about what?

3. What was against this Gentile woman?

4. Who were "the children" and who were "the dogs?"

5. What does the Greek word Jesus used for "dog" mean?

6. 6. What was bread used for in Jesus' day?

7. 7. What is significant about Jesus using the term "great faith?"

Chapter 21

"The 9000 and 19 Full Baskets"
Mark 8:14-21

And they had forgotten to take bread, and did not have more than one loaf in the boat with them. ¹⁵ And He was giving orders to them, saying, "Watch out! Beware of the leaven of the Pharisees and the leaven of Herod." ¹⁶ They began to discuss with one another the fact that they had no bread. ¹⁷ And Jesus, aware of this, said to them, "Why do you discuss the fact that you have no bread? Do you not yet see or understand? Do you have a hardened heart? ¹⁸ HAVING EYES, DO YOU NOT SEE? AND HAVING EARS, DO YOU NOT HEAR? And do you not remember ¹⁹ when I broke the five loaves for the five thousand, how many baskets full of broken pieces you picked up?" They said to Him, "Twelve." ²⁰ "When I broke the seven for the four thousand, how many large baskets full of broken pieces did you pick up?" And they said to Him, "Seven." ²¹ And He was saying to them, "Do you not yet understand?"

INTRODUCTION

IT WAS OPENING DAY OF trout season. Clem was walking down a lane carrying his fishing pole over his shoulder. The game warden stopped him and asked to see his fishing license. Clem stared back at him and said, "There ain't no law against carrying a fishing rod." The game warden knew he couldn't do anything. He watched Clem turn and walk into the woods. He waited for him to get aways ahead and started following him trying to be careful so Clem wouldn't know he was following him. Clem walked up a steep hill, crawled under a barbed wire fence on his belly, waded through a shallow stream, slid down a patch of gravel, stepped over an electric cow fence, and walked a few more miles with the exhausted game warden following, not so inconspicuously now. Finally, Clem came to a stream, waded in and baited his hook. As soon as he cast his line into the water the game warden excitedly popped out of the bushes and said, "Ah, now you are fishing! Let me see your license." Clem fired back without any hesitation, "And now you may see my fishing license."

This lesson is about fish and about bread. Do you remember Jesus feeding the 5,000 with 5 loaves and 2 fish? Just prior to this text, Jesus feeds the 4,000 with 7 loaves and a few fish. But this message is not about that. It focuses on the application Jesus is trying to make with the disciples to some of the events that have been taking place in His ministry.

After a confrontation with the Pharisees who were looking for a sign to accuse Him, Jesus and the disciples got into a boat and are heading back across the Sea of Galilee to Bethsaida. In their hurry to get on their way the disciples forgot to take any food. All they have is one loaf (verse 14). They are worried about what they are going to eat. Jesus uses this boat trip to teach some important lessons to the disciples. Let's look at some of the lessons Jesus taught.

JESUS CARES ABOUT ALL PEOPLE

The 5000 (or 10,000) Jesus fed with the 5 loaves and 2 fish were mostly Jews. The 4000 Jesus fed with 7 loaves and a few small fish were mostly Gentiles.

Jesus saw that everyone was filled (the 4000 had not eaten for 3 days) and there were leftovers. Jesus is the model of compassion for us to follow.

JESUS WAS WILLING TO RETURN TO THOSE WHO REJECTED HIM

The feeding of the 4000 took place in the area where Jesus had healed the Gaderene demoniac. Mark 5:17 says these people asked Jesus to leave their region. Perhaps the witness of this former demon possessed man had made a difference.

We should never underestimate the power of what one person can do. We should not be afraid to give people a second chance.

JESUS WANTS US TO SEE AND HEAR HIM

The disciples were talking among themselves about not having any bread. How sad that they were dealing with trivial matters when they were in the presence of Jesus.

Jesus must be disappointed with us when we do not see and hear what He wants us to see and hear. Twice in this text Jesus tells the disciples that they don't see or hear. They do not understand what He is really all about.

JESUS CAN TAKE LITTLE AND MAKE IT MUCH

He took 5 loaves and 2 fish and fed 5000 with 12 baskets of leftovers. He took 7 loaves and a few small fish and fed 4000 with 7 baskets of leftovers

The disciples were talking about only having one loaf of bread. All the while they had the Bread of Life in their midst in the boat. If Jesus could feed so many with so little, He surely could feed the twelve with one loaf.

JESUS KNOWS HOW TO DEAL WITH THE ENEMY

The Pharisees were looking for a sign. They didn't need one – Jesus was right there. Jesus didn't waste a lot of time arguing when He knew it wouldn't matter. He simply left and went to the other side of the Sea of Galilee.

Jesus warned the disciples to beware of the "leaven" of the enemy. "Leaven" here means the false teachings.

JESUS IS MOST CONCERNED ABOUT OUR SPIRITUAL CONDITION

Jesus met physical needs but it was always because He wanted to teach spiritual lessons and meet spiritual needs. If Jesus can perform miracles like feeding the 9000, imagine what He can do with the person that trusts Him and is committed to Him!

The disciples knew the facts. They could answer Jesus' questions, but they had not yet learned what the facts meant. "Do you not YET understand?" (Verse 21).

CONCLUSION

The 9000 and 19 baskets of leftovers teach us about the power of God. Do you understand how powerful God is?

The Christian believers in a Bolivia mining town were dedicating their new church building. They were a poor church and had constructed their church building from largely donated lumber and boards they had scavenged. The floor and some of the furniture were made from wooden shipping crates that explosives had come in for the local mine. When the preacher stepped to the pulpit he laid his Bible down on a piece of the crate where the words were still readable. Under his Bible were the words - "Danger- Explosives!"

Power is from the Greek word that we translate "dynamite" in English. The power is from God to smash evil and blow sin away. Romans 1:16 says we should not be ashamed of the Gospel because it is the power (dynamite) of God.

Do you get what Jesus is teaching? Or do you not yet understand?

Think on these things!

Discussion Questions

1. What was Jesus hoping to find out after the feeding of the 5,000 and the 4,000?

2. What did the disciples have to eat?

3. What was different about the feeding of the 4,000 from the feeding of the 5,000?

4. What did Jesus say the disciples didn't do twice in this lesson?

5. What did Jesus say the disciples should be aware of in the enemy?

6. Why do you think Jesus met people's physical needs?

7. What did Jesus want the disciples and us to learn from the feeding of the 9,000 and the 19 baskets of leftovers?

Chapter 22

"To the Unknown Servants"
Mark 8:22-26

And they came to Bethsaida. And they brought a blind man to Jesus and implored Him to touch him. ²³ Taking the blind man by the hand, He brought him out of the village; and after spitting on his eyes and laying His hands on him, He asked him, "Do you see anything?" ²⁴ And he looked up and said, "I see men, for I see them like trees, walking around." ²⁵ Then again He laid His hands on his eyes; and he looked intently and was restored, and began to see everything clearly. ²⁶ And He sent him to his home, saying, "Do not even enter the village."

INTRODUCTION

BLINDNESS IS A SCARY THING. We take our sight for granted. Most of us are familiar with blindness to some extent and know its difficulties. Several years ago, when I was dean of a Jr. Hi week of church camp, one of the activities we did was have half the kids be blindfolded and the other half be guides. The next day we switched. Our mission for the week was a blind mission. It was amazing how this demonstration affected the kids. The last day of camp we made the application to the kids of how spiritual blindness was even worse.

In this lesson I would like us to learn some things about spiritual blindness from physical blindness. I hope we will "SEE" how important it is to share the light with people. Jesus is the light of the world.

Our text is unique in that Mark is the only gospel writer who tells us of the healing of this blind man. Mark doesn't tell us who the individuals were that brought the blind man to Jesus. Even though we don't know who they were, they are important. Without them the man would not have been healed. These individuals were much like the four friends of the paralyzed man who was brought to Jesus. They lowered him down through the roof where Jesus was teaching inside a house. These individuals are "Unknown Servants!"

These "Unknown Servants" helped the blind man to "SEE."

Let's look at three words that spell "SEE."

SYMPATHETIC

The blind man was "brought" to Jesus (verse 22). We have to be willing to bring people to Jesus too. The people of Bethsaida had rejected Jesus. This man was not from this town. He seems to have just caught up with Jesus there.

Jesus took the man by the hand and took him outside the city to heal him. Why He did this we are not sure. Perhaps it was because Bethsaida had already judged Jesus and He didn't want to give them any more reason to accuse Him. Jesus had performed miracles there and they rejected Him (Matthew 11:21-24).

Jesus had sympathy on this blind man and healed him. We must have sympathy upon the spiritually blind so that it causes us to do something about it. Just feeling sorry is not enough. Those that brought the blind man to Jesus "entreated" Jesus to heal the man.

EMPATHETIC

Jesus healed the blind man in ways that he could understand. We must find common ground with people to share Jesus with them. This blind man had often been left out because he was blind. It is interesting that Jesus heals the man gradually. The Gospels tell of seven blind people being healed. Jesus used a variety of methods to heal them. We can help people see Jesus in a variety of ways.

Whatever the reason, the man was not ready for instant sight. Jesus had a way about Him that knew what a person needed. We need to try and empathize with the lost so we can best help them.

Jesus spit on his eyes and put His hands on him. The man evidently was not born blind because he recognized men and trees. A second time Jesus laid his hands upon the man and this time the man's eyes were restored and he saw clearly (verse 25).

ENERGETIC

The man was sent to his home after he could see so that he could witness to them of Jesus' saving power. He was warned though, not to go to Bethsaida (verse 26).

Sometimes conversion is dramatic and swift. Other times it can be a slow process. We must keep at it. We should not give up on someone who is slow on the path to conversion. We must always be energetic and upbeat as we try to help them SEE their need to come to the Lord.

We may be on the salvation train but we are not yet at the eternal station until we get to the end of the line. We must stay on the train to the end of the line.

We can't SEE or grasp all of God's truth at once. It takes time. It takes effort on our part. It takes energy!

CONCLUSION

Do you SEE anything? Sympathy, Empathy, Energy! We must be careful that we don't become blind ourselves and harden our hearts. Be the servant that takes someone else to Jesus. It could make all the difference in the world for that person.

Fanny Crosby became blind at the age of 6 months. She had no recollection of ever seeing anyone. She penned over 8000 gospel songs. Many of them we sing in church. Once a minister told her he thought it was a pity that Jesus hadn't healed her of her blindness when He had given her so many other blessings. She quickly responded, "If I would have been able at birth to make one petition it would have been to be born blind. You see, when I get to heaven the first face I will ever see will be that of my Lord and Savior, Jesus Christ."

Be a servant and help others SEE Jesus! Rescue the perishing, duty demands it.

Discussion Questions

1. Not being able to see is a tragedy. But what is even worse?

2. Why is the healing of the blind man unique?

3. What is the significance of the blind man's friends and what are they called?

4. What had the people of Bethsaida done?

5. What do the letters in "SEE" mean?

6. How do we know this man was not born blind?

7. What responsibility do we have to lost people?

Chapter 23

"Who Am I?"
Mark 8:27-33

Jesus went out, along with His disciples, to the village of Caesarea Philippi; and on the way He questioned His disciples, saying to them, "Who do people say that I am?" [28] *They told Him, saying, "John the Baptist; and others say Elijah; but others, one of the prophets."* [29] *And He continued by questioning them, "But who do you say that I am?" Peter answered and said to Him, "You are the Christ."* [30] *And He warned them to tell no one about Him.*

INTRODUCTION

SCIENTISTS WERE STUDYING THE IMPACT of a high cholesterol diet on heart disease. To measure the effects, they fed a group of genetically similar rabbits the same high cholesterol diet. To their amazement, half the rabbits developed heart trouble while the other half were normal with no apparent heart disease. The outcome was not explainable so they bought new rabbits and repeated the study. After two months the results were the same as before. Something was wrong with the research design but they didn't know what it was. Eventually they discovered that during the evening the student they hired to feed the rabbits took them out of the cage and cuddled and petted them and talked to them while she changed their bedding and refreshed their food and water. However, she was short and couldn't reach far enough back into the top row of cages to get the rabbits so they were all fed and cages cleaned without these rabbits being handled or touched. Sure enough, after two months, the top row of rabbits all had heart disease, while the bottom row that were held and loved were all healthy. The environment and diet were the same. The only variable was love expressed by touching.

In this text, we see that Jesus has touched the disciples for almost three years. He has taught them, showed them, and modeled the perfect life for them. But who do they think He really is? If Jesus asks, "Who am I?", what will the disciples answer? There is no more important question that Jesus asks than that. Who a person believes Jesus to be makes all the difference in the world. How a person answers that question will affect every decision that they make. Not everyone has the same view of who Jesus is that we do. Even in Jesus' day people had different opinions and ideas as to who He was when they saw Him.

"WHO AM I?" according to the PEOPLE

Some of the people thought Jesus was John the Baptist, Elijah or one of the other prophets. Why would people think Jesus was one of these?

Today, people think Jesus is a good teacher, a good man, an angel, a former TV evangelist, a crazy religious fanatic, or one of the many ways to get to heaven.

"WHO AM I?" according to the DISCIPLES

Who others say Jesus is really does not matter. Would the disciples see Jesus as other people do? Or would they see Him for who He really is?

Peter answers Jesus' question by saying, "You are the Christ." Matthew's account adds "the Son of the living God" (Matthew 16:16). Until now the disciples didn't understand who Jesus was. They didn't yet get it. But this is the defining moment when the light went on! This was the moment Jesus was waiting for.

Until they got that He was the Messiah, the Savior and Lord, Jesus could not proceed with revealing to them what was ahead for Him. He warned them not to tell anyone (verse 30) because He did not want to rush into the events that had to take place before the time came.

"WHO AM I?" according to YOU

The answer you give to this question is what really matters. Each of us has to answer that question. How others answer that question doesn't matter. How the disciples answered the question doesn't matter. Jesus wants to know what your answer is to that question.

Do you recognize Jesus as Messiah, Savior, Lord, and the Son of God? "Salvation is found in no one else, for there is no other name under heaven given to men by which we must be saved" (Acts 4:12).

There is only One Way! A lot of people and those who say there are many roads that lead to heaven are wrong. Jesus is "THE" way, "THE" truth and "THE" life. "No one comes to the Father except through Me", Jesus said in John 14:6. Unless you are in a church that teaches this, you are in the wrong church and you could be in danger of not making it to heaven yourself. Jesus said that we should seek to enter by the narrow gate because the path and gate is wide that leads to destruction (Matthew 7:13, 14).

CONCLUSION

Because the disciples finally realized who Jesus was, He could begin to tell them about His coming death and start preparing them for what would happen. Unless they understood who He was they would not be able to even begin to understand about His death and resurrection.

Verses 31-33 tell us what happens when we are ruled by the world's standards rather than by Christ. Listen to these words - "And He began to teach them that the Son of Man must suffer many things and be rejected by the elders and the chief priests and the scribes, and be killed, and after three days rise again. [32] And He was stating the matter plainly. And Peter took Him aside and began to rebuke Him. [33] But turning around and seeing His disciples, He rebuked Peter and said, "Get behind Me, Satan; for you are not setting your mind on God's interests, but man's."

Even though the disciples had just made the good confession about who Jesus was they still had their own interests that were ahead of God's interests (verse 33). We should never get in God's way like Peter did. That is why Jesus told Peter, "Get behind Me, Satan." We must always set our mind on the interests of God and not on our own or on other people's interests.

You and you alone must answer the question - "WHO DO YOU SAY THAT JESUS IS?"

Jesus is the Christ, the Son of the living God!

Discussion Questions

1. 1. Why did Jesus ask the disciples the question, "Who do you say that I am?"

2. What was Peter's answer to this question?

3. Who did the people say that Jesus was?

4. What is so important about how a person answers this question?

5. What does Matthew's account of this add to Peter's answer?

6. Why do you think Jesus called Peter "Satan"?

7. Who do you say Jesus is?

Chapter 24

"The Secret of Following Jesus"
Mark 8:34-38

And He summoned the crowd with His disciples, and said to them, "If anyone wishes to come after Me, he must deny himself, and take up his cross and follow Me. ³⁵ For whoever wishes to save his life will lose it, but whoever loses his life for My sake and the gospel's will save it. ³⁶ For what does it profit a man to gain the whole world, and forfeit his soul? ³⁷ For what will a man give in exchange for his soul? ³⁸ For whoever is ashamed of Me and My words in this adulterous and sinful generation, the Son of Man will also be ashamed of him when He comes in the glory of His Father with the holy angels."

INTRODUCTION

THE INFLUENCE OF CHRIST HAS a far-reaching affect on life. Consider Max Jukes and Jonathan Edwards. Someone studied these two men's family trees. Here is what was found:

Max Jukes- 900 descendants   Jonathan Edwards- 729 descendants
(Max- lazy and not religious)   (Jonathan was a devout Christian)
300 delinquents   300 preachers

200 died early deaths	65 college professors
145 drunks	13 college presidents
285 various diseases	60 authors of good books
90 prostitutes	3 US congressmen
100 convicts (avg. 13 years)	1 US Vice President

There must be something to the influence Christ has on a life. When we know who Jesus is, there comes a point in time when we must make a decision as to whether we are going to follow Him or not. Matthew records Jesus' simple invitation with these words: "Follow Me." Jesus calls all of us to follow Him. Some people do. Some try but get lost in the "woulds" like "I *would* follow Jesus but…!"

There is a chorus by Danny Stutzman that I like. It goes like this: "Follow Jesus, I will follow Jesus. Anywhere He leads me I will follow. Follow Jesus, I will follow Jesus. Anywhere He leads I'll go. Across the river, down through the valley, or if it be on the mountain high, I'll go, Lord, anywhere You want me, take me, here am I."

In our text, Jesus was asking the disciples and us if there is a cross in our future. You see, there can be no crown without the cross. There is a price to pay for being a true follower of Jesus Christ. Jesus knew that the crowds, for the most part, were only following Him because of His miracles. Most of them would not be willing to pay the price for following Him. The secret of following Jesus is seen in the three conditions of a true follower.

COMPLETE SURRENDER TO CHRIST

To follow Christ, we must first make the decision that we are going to deny ourselves. Denying self is not the same as self denial. Self denial is when we give up things and activities. Denying self means to surrender completely to Christ and obey His will for our lives.

We say no to self and yes to Christ. We lose ourselves to gain Christ. WWJD! What would Jesus do! It is no longer I that lives but Christ living in me. When we live for Christ, we become more like Him.

COMPLETE IDENTIFICATION WITH CHRIST

We willingly pick up our cross and carry it. Our cross can be anything that keeps us from following the Lord. It might be that one area that in which we are hesitant to give total surrender to the Lord.

We each have a cross to bear. It may be family, an apathetic spouse, a failed marriage, a blended family, trials and temptations, or worldly influences.

Jesus does not ask us to do anything that He Himself hasn't already done. He can identify with us because He has been there. Cross bearing is voluntary! We must want to pick up our cross. We must want to wear His name. We must want to live His Life. We can't be ashamed of Jesus (verse 38).

In Luke 9:23 we have this same account. Luke adds the word "daily" in his telling of this event. Every day we must choose to take up our cross and identify with Christ or we will be identified with the world.

COMPLETE OBEDIENCE TO CHRIST

Will we waste our lives or will we invest them for the Lord? To lose your soul is to waste the life you have been given. We cannot follow Jesus unless we obey Him. Obedience demands a growing knowledge of what He wants us to do. Ignorance will not be an excuse God will accept.

It is not, "I will follow Jesus as long as he leads me where I want to go!" It Is, "Follow Jesus, anywhere He leads me." Jesus does not force us to follow Him. He invites us to follow Him. It is up to us to accept His invitation.

We must make the most of the opportunities we have here on earth. God gives us a great opportunity so that we can be with Him for all eternity. All we need to do is obey Him. If we lose ourselves we will find ourselves. If we lose our life for Christ we will find ourselves saved.

CONCLUSION

We are no fool when we willingly give up that which we cannot keep to gain that which we cannot lose. Giving up my desires is okay because they get replaced with His desires. Are you willing to live for Jesus and be always pure and good? Would you let Him have His way with you?

Mt. 10:32,33 says, "Therefore, everyone who confesses Me before men, I will also confess him before My Father who is in heaven. ³³ But whoever denies Me before men, I will also deny him before My Father who is in heaven." This is the secret of following Jesus.

Discussion Questions

1. What can Christ's influence do for us?

2. There can't be a crown without what?

3. What three conditions does a true follower of Jesus have?

4. Cross bearing is what?

5. What do we have to do to gain Christ?

6. Where will you follow Jesus?

7. Is there a cross and a crown in your future?

Chapter 25

"All Things are Possible"
Mark 9:14-29

became so much like a corpse that most *of them* said, "He is dead!" [27] But Jesus took him by the hand and raised him; and he got up. [28] When He came into *the* house, His disciples *began* questioning *When they came back to the disciples, they saw a large crowd around them, and some scribes arguing with them.* [15] *Immediately, when the entire crowd saw Him, they were amazed and began running up to greet Him.* [16] *And He asked them, "What are you discussing with them?"* [17] *And one of the crowd answered Him, "Teacher, I brought You my son, possessed with a spirit which makes him mute;* [18] *and whenever it seizes him, it slams him to the ground and he foams at the mouth, and grinds his teeth and stiffens out. I told Your disciples to cast it out, and they could not do it."* [19] *And He answered them and said, "O unbelieving generation, how long shall I be with you? How long shall I put up with you? Bring him to Me!"* [20] *They brought the boy to Him. When he saw Him, immediately the spirit threw him into a convulsion, and falling to the ground, he began rolling around and foaming at the mouth.* [21] *And He asked his father, "How long has this been happening to him?" And he said, "From childhood.* [22] *It has often thrown him both into the fire and into the water to destroy*

him. But if You can do anything, take pity on us and help us!"
²³ And Jesus said to him, "'If You can?' All things are possible to
him who believes." ²⁴ Immediately the boy's father cried out and
said, "I do believe; help my unbelief." ²⁵ When Jesus saw that
a crowd was rapidly gathering, He rebuked the unclean spirit,
saying to it, "You deaf and mute spirit, I command you, come
out of him and do not enter him again." ²⁶ After crying out and
throwing him into terrible convulsions, it came out; and the boy
Him privately, "Why could we not drive it out?" ²⁹ And He said
to them, "This kind cannot come out by anything but prayer."

INTRODUCTION

HAVE YOU EVER HAD A mountain top experience one day and then
been in the valley the next day? It is tough when you are sailing along
through life and out of nowhere the wind gets knocked out of your sails.

Just before our text Jesus had taken Peter, James and John up on a mountain.
While they were there, what we call the "Transfiguration" took place. Elijah and
Moses, who were dead, appeared and conversed with Jesus whose appearance
became radiant and bright. The word "transfiguration" means metamorphosis.
The change in Jesus and the experience so moved Peter, James and John that
they wanted to build special tabernacles for Jesus, Elijah and Moses to make a
place to worship and remember their mountain top experience.

Jesus, of course, did not allow it. Jesus, Peter, James and John came down
the mountain to where the other nine disciples were waiting. Jesus was met by
a crowd that was discussing why the nine disciples could not heal the epileptic
boy. Verse 15 indicates that the crowd ran up to Jesus. They probably were
wondering if Jesus could heal the boy when the nine disciples could not. Let's
look at the failure and the success that took place here.

The Disciples Failure

Can you imagine how the nine disciples felt when Jesus took Peter, James
and John up the mountain and left them behind? It also seems that the
religious leaders may have been making fun of the disciples for their failure
to heal the boy.

The boy had an evil spirit from childhood that dashed him to the ground, made him foam at the mouth, grind his teeth, become stiff and rigid, go into convulsions, and sometimes the evil spirit threw him into the fire or water.

The nine disciples seem to have been careless with their Christianity. They had become lazy in their spiritual walk. Jesus gave them authority but it was only effective when administered in faith. Jesus says they failed to cast out the evil spirit because they did not pray and, some manuscripts add, fast (verse 29).

Faith must be cultivated by spiritual discipline and devotion to Christ. The nine disciples must have been in the valley when they failed to heal the boy.

Jesus Never Fails

Jesus was upset at the people for their lack of faith. He even called them an "unbelieving generation". He told them to bring the boy to Him in verse 19. When they did, the evil spirit caused the boy to have a seizure.

The boy's father said to Jesus, "If You can do anything, have pity on us and help us" (verse 22). Jesus' comeback seems to show His disappointment. He said, "If You can! All things are possible to him who believes" (verse 23).

The boys father cried out in response, "I do believe, help me in my unbelief" (verse 24). Jesus saw the crowd getting bigger so he rebuked the unclean spirit and it came out of the boy and he became like a corpse and the people thought he was dead until Jesus took him by the hand and helped him up.

What a difference a Savior makes!

CONCLUSION

Jesus not only helped this boy, his father and the crowd, He also helped the disciples who had failed see their need for a closer spiritual walk with the Savior. He increased everyone's faith by showing them they needed to pray and fast. Jesus never fails. With Him, all things are possible if we believe.

Our prayer should be that of the boy's father: "I do believe, help me in my unbelief."

The fields were parched and brown from a lack of rain. Crops lay wilted from thirst in the fields. People were anxious and irritable as they searched the sky for any sign of the hope of rain. There had been no rain for so long that the local church ministers got together and called for a special time of prayer in the town square. They requested that everyone come at the appointed time and bring an object of faith and inspiration. At the appointed time, almost everyone came. Some brought books, Bibles, crosses and rosaries. Prayers were offered for an hour. As the last prayer was being said a soft gentle rain began to fall. Cheers went up from the crowd and they held their treasured items of inspiration high in gratitude and praise.

From the middle of the crowd one faith symbol seemed to overshadow all the other. A nine-year-old child had brought an umbrella! -from "Chicken Soup for the Christian Soul" by Laverne W. Hall

Do you believe all things are possible with God?

Discussion Questions

1. What do you know about the "Transfiguration"?

2. Why couldn't the 9 disciples heal the epileptic boy?

3. How do we cultivate faith?

4. What did Jesus call these people and why?

5. What did the boy's father cry out?

6. Who did Jesus help in this text?

7. Do you believe all things are possible with God?

Chapter 26

"Who is the Greatest?"
Mark 9: 30-37

From there they went out and began to go through Galilee, and He did not want anyone to know about it. ³¹ For He was teaching His disciples and telling them, "The Son of Man is to be delivered into the hands of men, and they will kill Him; and when He has been killed, He will rise three days later." ³² But they did not understand this statement, and they were afraid to ask Him.

³³ They came to Capernaum; and when He was in the house, He began to question them, "What were you discussing on the way?" ³⁴ But they kept silent, for on the way they had discussed with one another which of them was the greatest. ³⁵ Sitting down, He called the twelve and said to them, "If anyone wants to be first, he shall be last of all and servant of all." ³⁶ Taking a child, He set him before them, and taking him in His arms, He said to them, ³⁷ "Whoever receives one child like this in My name receives Me; and whoever receives Me does not receive Me, but Him who sent Me."

INTRODUCTION

OLYMPIC COMPETITION HAPPENS EVERY FOUR years. The competition for greatness to get the gold medal draws our attention pretty well. In our text, there was some competition going on among the disciples about which one of them was the greatest. We see that the disciples were human just like us. As they were walking they were talking about who was the greatest among themselves. Perhaps this discussion was started by Peter, James or John who had went with Jesus to the mount of Transfiguration. The mount of transfiguration was about 55 miles from Jerusalem (a two-day walk).

This dispute among the disciples is well attested as it appears in all four Gospels. It seems that they tried to keep their discussion from Jesus because when He asks them what they were talking about on the journey, verse 34 says they kept quiet.

As Jesus' time was drawing closer He wanted to teach them the importance of having honor and humility. In this lesson we want to look at greatness by looking at its desire, difficulty and discipline.

THE DESIRE FOR GREATNESS (verse 34)

It is a universal desire for a person to want to be great. We all want to be great. We all want our 15 minutes of fame. Some even want to be great at not being great. Success is programmed into us. We want to accomplish something with our life. We desire to make a difference.

In our desire for greatness there are dangers. Sometimes we use other people to get ahead and then throw them away when we get ahead. Our seeking to be great, famous, a success or whatever, tends to divide rather than unify us. Our desire for greatness causes us to have unhealthy rivalries.

Our desire for greatness sometimes makes us pretty selfish. We only look out for ourselves. We tend to focus on self. We may even have the desire in competition to win so that we will do whatever we can get away with to win. We may want the team to win but we want the glory. Decisions are made on the basis of whether we get ahead or not.

The desire to be great is a good desire but how we deal with it often is not good. The desire to be great can be a good motivator.

THE DIFFICULTY OF GREATNESS (verse 35)

The difficulty of greatness is that it is ironic. Sometimes it is just the opposite of what we think it should be. It is paradoxical - contrary to what is common sense. For example: to be first you must be last. To be honored you must be humble. To be great you must be the least. The way to be last is to not serve others.

The qualities of greatness are seen in Jesus. He was rich - yet He became poor. He left the glories of heaven to come to the worldliness of this earth. He left a heavenly home with His Father to come to the world where He had no place to even lay his head.

It is our natural tendency to want to be first. Just watch kids line up for lunch, ice cream or whatever! It isn't easy to think in spiritual terms. It is a constant battle. The old man of sin keeps getting in our way to greatness.

THE DISCIPLINE OF GREATNESS (verse 36)

Jesus uses an object lesson to teach us how to have honor and be great. Jesus knew all along what the disciples had been discussing on their journey to Capernaum. Jesus sits down and calls the disciples over to join Him. He says, "If anyone wants to be first, he shall be last of all, and servant of all" (verse 35).

To illustrate this, He took a child and stood him in the middle of them. A child has honest acceptance, an eagerness to learn, and is moldable. A child is an example of submission and humility.

Children were the lowest on the social scale. It was men, women and then children in order of importance. Children were to be seen not heard. In fact, according to Jewish tradition, you weren't considered worthy of being listened to until you were 30 years of age. That is why Jesus didn't begin His ministry until he was 30.

The disciples were acting like anything but a child in their desire to be great. Jesus said that if the disciples wanted to be really great they would have to accept and treat people and each other like a child. If they accepted people like a child they were accepting Him. Listen to what verse 37 says: "Whoever receives one child like this in My name receives Me; and whoever receives Me does not receive Me, but Him who sent Me."

CONCLUSION

True humility means you know yourself and you give yourself in service to others. The world says you are great if you have others working for you. Jesus says you are great when you serve others. The words "child" and "servant" are the same in the Aramaic language that Jesus spoke. If we have the heart of a child then we will serve others. If we have the attitude of a servant then we will be like a child.

We should not think more highly of ourselves than we ought to. Jesus said in Matthew 18:3, "Unless you are converted and become like children, you shall not enter the kingdom of heaven."

How much like a child are you in your faith? Being like a child is the way to greatness!

Discussion Questions

1. 1. What were the disciples talking about that they didn't want Jesus to know about?

2. Why do you think this account is found in all four of the Gospels?

3. What does our desire for greatness cause us to do?

4. What is ironic about our desire to be great?

5. What was the object lesson that Jesus used to teach the disciples about greatness?

6. In Jesus' day, where did children fit into the social scene?

7. What word is similar to child in Aramaic?

Chapter 27

"For Better or For Worse"
Mark 10:1-12

*Getting up, He went from there to the region of Judea and beyond the Jordan; crowds gathered around Him again, and, according to His custom, He once more began to teach them.
²Some Pharisees came up to Jesus, testing Him, and began to question Him whether it was lawful for a man to divorce a wife. ³And He answered and said to them, "What did Moses command you?"⁴They said, "Moses permitted a man TO WRITE A CERTIFICATE OF DIVORCE AND SEND her AWAY." ⁵But Jesus said to them, "Because of your hardness of heart he wrote you this commandment. ⁶But from the beginning of creation, God MADE THEM MALE AND FEMALE. ⁷FOR THIS REASON A MAN SHALL LEAVE HIS FATHER AND MOTHER, ⁸AND THE TWO SHALL BECOME ONE FLESH; so they are no longer two, but one flesh. ⁹What therefore God has joined together, let no man separate." ¹⁰In the house the disciples began questioning Him about this again. ¹¹And He said to them, "Whoever divorces his wife and marries another woman commits adultery against her; ¹²and if she herself divorces her husband and marries another man, she is committing adultery."*

INTRODUCTION

A YOUNG BOY WENT TO THE preacher and asked him why a man could have 16 wives. The minister wasn't sure why the boy would ask that so he asked him what he meant. The boy replied, "We went to this wedding yesterday and the minister said, 4 better, 4 worse, 4 richer and 4 poorer. That is 16 isn't it?"

Our text is about divorce, a very touchy subject. It is not an easy subject or a popular one but it is an important subject. I don't claim to have all the answers, but I do know what the Bible says and what Jesus has said about it. Divorce is far too common today. In many cases it has become easier to get a divorce than to try to work it out. The family and home suffer because of divorce. The tragedy of divorce is that it affects so many people for the rest of their lives.

Maybe the reason divorce has become such a problem is because we have gotten away from God's intended plan.

The Testing Question (verse 2)

"Is it lawful for a man to divorce his wife?" The motive for the Pharisees question was to test Jesus. They wanted to know where He stood on the issue. Divorce was a sticky situation to which there was no easy answer even in Jesus' day. According to John the Baptist, Herod had divorced his wife so he could live with his brother, Phillip's, wife. The Pharisees knew the Law of Moses and were trying to catch Jesus going against what Moses' law taught.

Deuteronomy 24:1 says that a man could divorce his wife for any reason that displeased him. He could give her a certificate of divorce and send her on her way.

There were two interpretations or schools of thought on this promoted by two Jewish religious leaders of Jesus' day. First, was the school of Shimmai who taught the strict belief that only adultery was reason for permitting divorce. The second school of thought was the liberal view taught by Hillel. They taught that divorce was permitted for almost any reason. If you burnt a meal, talked to a stranger, talked back to your husband, wore the wrong clothes, you could get a certificate of divorce.

No matter how Jesus answered the question about divorce He was going to make one of these schools of thought angry.

Jesus' Inspired Answer (verses 3-9)

Jesus smartly asked them what Moses had commanded. Everyone knew that Moses permitted divorce because of the hardness of man's heart.

Jesus says that there should not be divorce, but God allows it anyway because He loves us. Jesus is saying that Moses' statement permitting divorce was God's attempt at controlling the problem.

Jesus responds by going back in time before Moses' command to allow divorce. Jesus goes all the way back to creation to show that Moses was only offering a temporary solution for divorce. From the beginning it was not a part of God's original plan.

Jesus shows us that His desire for marriage was for one man and one woman to be in a permanent loving relationship until they were parted by death. But Jesus does permit divorce even though He hates it, because He loves people.

The Point for Today

As we wrestle with the question of divorce today we often miss the real point. Whatever God has joined together, no one should separate. Love, sex and marriage should be seen in the serious spiritual light that God has revealed to us.

Spiritual adultery is something God has been dealing with ever since Adam and Eve sinned in the Garden of Eden. Adultery is when we put anything before our love for God. God's plan was for Adam and Eve to be with Him in a sinless world forever. But sin caused God to turn to plan B.

God's plan was for the children of Israel to go directly to the Promised Land, but because of sin they wandered for 40 years in the wilderness. God's plan A for marriage is for a man and a woman to leave their mother and father and to become one and remain faithful to each other for their lifetimes. But often, because of sin, God allows for plan B, or should I say plan "D" for divorce.

God's plan is always the best plan. But because God loves us He allows less perfect plans to exist and be permitted in our lives. Adultery and divorce are forgivable. There are many complications that affect so many and make it difficult but God will help us if we find ourselves in such a situation. God is in the business of loving and helping sinners. Jesus told the woman caught in adultery He didn't condemn her. But He told her to go her way and sin no more.

We should do everything we can to prevent divorce. But if divorce has come to us or is close by it is so important to let the love of God bring forgiveness, healing and hope. As a church we hate divorce but we are here to love people no matter what. After all, none of us are worthy to cast the first stone.

CONCLUSION

God's desire is for the better to be our life. But even if the worse becomes our life His love for us will never change The point Jesus wanted people to see was that a Godly marriage was the ideal situation He desired. But when that was not possible, He permitted divorce.

A soldier was coming home after the war and called home from San Francisco. He asked his parents if he could bring a buddy home to live with them. This buddy had stepped on a landmine and lost an arm and a leg. The parents weren't too anxious for him to bring his buddy home with him. They expressed their displeasure in that and asked him to come home alone even though they had the room. They just didn't want all the inconvenience that taking care of his buddy would cause.

The son hung up the phone and the parents waited for several days but their son didn't arrive. One day the parents received a call from the San Francisco police. They were notified that their son had fallen off a building and apparently committed suicide. They quickly flew across the country to identify his body and bring him back for burial. They recognized him at the morgue but to their horror found that he was missing one arm and leg.

We are like those parents sometimes. It is easy to love the lovely but we don't want to be bothered or inconvenienced by those who are less lovely or healthy or down on their luck or divorced. We would rather stay away from those people. Thankfully Jesus didn't think that way. He is in the business of loving and forgiving.

Jesus doesn't seek perfect people. He came to seek and to save the lost. Regardless of your marital status Jesus loves you and the church should love you too!

Discussion Questions

1. What is the tragedy of divorce?

2. Why do you think divorce has become such a problem today?

3. What was the question the Pharisees asked Jesus and why did they ask it?

4. What did Moses say about divorce?

5. How did Jesus get around what Moses said?

6. Why does God allow plan "B"?

7. What should be our response to someone who is divorced?

Chapter 28

"Eternal Life Within Your Grasp"
Mark 10:17-22

As Jesus was setting out on a journey, a man ran up to Him and knelt before Him, and asked Him, "Good Teacher, what shall I do to inherit eternal life?" [18] And Jesus said to him, "Why do you call Me good? No one is good except God alone. [19] You know the commandments, 'DO NOT MURDER, DO NOT COMMIT ADULTERY, DO NOT STEAL, DO NOT BEAR FALSE WITNESS, Do not defraud, HONOR YOUR FATHER AND MOTHER.'" [20] And he said to Him, "Teacher, I have kept all these things from my youth up." [21] Looking at him, Jesus felt a love for him and said to him, "One thing you lack: go and sell all you possess and give to the poor, and you will have treasure in heaven; and come, follow Me." [22] But at these words he was saddened, and he went away grieving, for he was one who owned much property.

INTRODUCTION

IT WAS SATURDAY NIGHT OF Thanksgiving weekend and the Cocoanut Grove was packed. Waiters were setting up extra tables to handle the diners. The overflow from the dining room surged down a narrow stairway to the Melody Lounge. This dimly lit basement bar offered a South Seas ambiance, with artificial palm trees, driftwood, rattan and a ceiling draped in blue satin. The only illumination came from behind the bar, supplemented by low-wattage bulbs hidden in the palms. Even this was too bright for one young man. He reached up, unscrewed a bulb and settled back in his date's arms. Like many others there, he was in uniform. It was 1942; the U.S. had been fighting WWII for nearly a year. Dr. Vincent Senna was having dinner that night in the Grove and was paged because one of his patients had gone into labor. Grumbling, Senna rushed to the hospital in time to deliver the baby...and save his life. Because after he left, for still unknown reasons, the Cocoanut Grove burst into flames, and over 490 people died in the smoke and flames. The interruption that ruined his evening also saved his life! *Reader's Digest*, Nov, 1992.

Our text has an interruption in it. We need to see that Jesus saw the interruptions as a ministry opportunity rather than being upset that His plans were altered. The rich young ruler came to Jesus and interrupted Him with this question: "Good Teacher, what shall I do to have eternal life?

Knowing God is not Enough

The rich young ruler knew enough about God to find Jesus. He came to Jesus and knelt before Him. He addressed Jesus as "Good Teacher." He asked the right question - "What must I do to have eternal life?" He had obeyed what he knew - the Ten Commandments. He had obeyed the commandments from his youth up (verse 20).

Being Good is not Enough

The rich young ruler thought he should go to heaven because he was a good person. There are many people today that think they are good enough to go to heaven.

The problem is that doing good things does not make us good. Jesus points out to the rich young ruler and to us that no one is good but God (verse 18). We will never be good enough to get into heaven.

We might be good if we could keep all the commandments, but we can't. Jesus looked at the rich young ruler and loved him. He told him that there was one thing he lacked to do to have eternal life - "Go and sell your possessions and give it to the poor, and you shall have treasures in heaven; and come, follow Me" (verse 21). The rich young ruler's claim that he had kept all the commandments was a lie.

The Heart of the Matter

Which of the commandments does our text reveal that he had not kept from his youth up? It is the first commandment - to have no other gods before the Lord.

The rich young ruler put his riches before God because he was not willing to sell his possessions and give the money to the poor. When he heard Jesus tell him to do that, verse 22 says his face fell. He was sad and went away grieved because he had much property.

The rich young ruler had the misunderstanding that he was good enough to go to heaven. He had been deceived because none of us are good enough to go to heaven on our own.

We all need Jesus. We must trust Him and obey him. Jesus asked the rich young ruler to do the one thing that really kept him from having eternal life.

I have always liked to think that if the rich young ruler would have been willing to go and sell his possessions that the Lord would have stopped him much like He stopped Abraham from killing Isaac on the alter once He saw his obedience.

The Need for Grace

The rich young ruler seemed to have it all on the surface. He, like many today, believe they will go to heaven because they are good.

The word "grieved" in verse 22 gives us the picture of gathering storm clouds. The rich young ruler had eternal life within his grasp but he didn't grab it. Instead he walked from the sunshine into the storm.

On our own we will never be good enough. We need God's amazing grace. The rich young ruler refused God's grace.

That is why Jesus said it was easier for a camel to go through the eye of a needle than for a rich man to inherit eternal life (verse 25).

With man it is impossible to get eternal life, but with God all things are possible (verse 27). What does it profit a man to gain the whole world and forfeit his soul?

CONCLUSION

How tragic to have eternal life so close to you but fail to accept it. In Acts 2, people asked what they had to do to have eternal life and they were told to repent and be baptized. They did and about 3,000 were saved that day because they obeyed. The rich young ruler could have been saved too, but he decided not to obey. We can only hope that later on he changed his mind. But we have no record in the Bible that he did.

You can have eternal life if you will obey the commands of the Lord. Eternal life is within your grasp. Will you grab it right now?

Discussion Questions

1. How did Jesus look at interruptions?

2. What question did the rich young ruler ask Jesus and what did he call Jesus?

3. Who is good?

4. What commandment do we know the rich young ruler had not kept and why?

5. What does the word "grieved" mean?

6. What did Jesus say when the rich young ruler refused God's grace?

7. How could the rich young ruler have had eternal life?

Chapter 29

"The Leading Characteristic of a Leader"
Mark 10:35-45

James and John, the two sons of Zebedee, came up to Jesus, saying, "Teacher, we want You to do for us whatever we ask of You." ³⁶ And He said to them, "What do you want Me to do for you?" ³⁷ They said to Him, "Grant that we may sit, one on Your right and one on Your left, in Your glory." ³⁸ But Jesus said to them, "You do not know what you are asking. Are you able to drink the cup that I drink, or to be baptized with the baptism with which I am baptized?" ³⁹ They said to Him, "We are able." And Jesus said to them, "The cup that I drink you shall drink; and you shall be baptized with the baptism with which I am baptized. ⁴⁰ But to sit on My right or on My left, this is not Mine to give; but it is for those for whom it has been prepared." ⁴¹ Hearing this, the ten began to feel indignant with James and John. ⁴² Calling them to Himself, Jesus said to them, "You know that those who are recognized as rulers of the Gentiles lord it over them; and their great men exercise authority over them. ⁴³ But it is not this way among you, but whoever wishes to become great among you shall be your servant; ⁴⁴ and whoever wishes to be first among you shall be slave of all. ⁴⁵ For even the

Son of Man did not come to be served, but to serve, and to give
His life a ransom for many.

INTRODUCTION

THIS LESSON CONTAINS THE VERSE we are using as our theme
verse for this book - Mark 10:45: "For even the Son of man did not come
to be served but to serve, and to give His life a ransom for many."

The leading characteristic of a leader is that they are servants first. You
can't be a real leader unless you are a servant first. You can be a servant without
being a leader but you can't be a leader without being a servant.

Background

The disciples that had followed Jesus were confused because when they
followed Jesus they expected something much different than what they were
getting. This text is the third announcement that Jesus makes of His coming
death. The other two were Mark 8:31 and Mark 9:31. This time He also
tells them where His death will occur - in Jerusalem (verse 33).

James and John ask Jesus for the seats on His right and left in glory. This
seems to be a continuation of the disciples' earlier discussion about which one
of them was the greatest (Mark 9:33-37).

In Matthew's account of this, (Matthew 20:20-28), he says James' and
John's mother, Salome, brings her sons to Jesus and she asks Jesus to grant
that her sons sit on the right and the left of Jesus.

Regardless of who did the asking, it seems to have been a planned-out
request. The disciples just don't seem to understand the meaning of the cross.
The request was made from selfish motives that were wrong. No leader can
be a good leader if they are looking out for themselves first.

Baptism and the Cup

Jesus said they didn't realize what they were asking. He compared His
coming suffering and death to drinking a cup and baptism. To follow him

they would have to drink the cup He was drinking and be baptized with the baptism He was being baptized with.

It would be a devastating experience to go through. The cup represented dying to self, suffering and even giving up your life. Baptism represented becoming fully immersed in God's will and being righteous even to the point of death. (Luke 12:50)

James and John say they are willing to drink the cup and be baptized but they didn't really know what they were saying. But later they would experience the cup and baptism Jesus was referring to.

James would become the first of the apostles to die for his faith as he was put to death with a sword by Herod. John would undergo persecution also and be banished to the isle of Patmos. Their request and desire for power and prestige caused anger and division among the disciples (verse 41), just the opposite of what Jesus was looking for as His time drew closer to going to the cross.

Becoming a Servant

Lording it over others or exercising authority over others is not the way to become a leader. The disciples were following the example of the Roman rulers who they thought were important because of their power and position.

Instead of modeling the Romans, they should have been modeling Jesus. There is nothing wrong with wanting to be great if our definition of "greatness" is correct. Jesus says, "…whoever wishes to become great among you shall be your servant and whoever wishes to be first among you shall be slave of all" (Mark 10:43,44).

Jesus is our example. We must become a servant like Him. That is the leading characteristic of a leader.

CONCLUSION

We have to be able to follow orders before we are worthy to give them. We must prove ourselves under the authority of others before we can exercise authority over others.

Becoming a servant starts with having a right relationship with Jesus and continues by having a servant's heart and attitude in all we say and do as we fulfill the Lord's will for our lives. Living the life of a servant ends with the words, "Well done you good and faithful servant."

Discussion Questions

1. What is the leading characteristic of a leader?

2. Finish this sentence: You can be a servant without being a leader but you can't be -?

3. How many times had Jesus told the disciples about His death now?

4. What did James and John ask Jesus that made the other disciples angry?

5. What two things would James and John have to do to follow Jesus?

6. Instead of modeling leadership after the Romans, who should the disciples have been modeling?

7. How does becoming a servant begin and continue?

Chapter 30

"Have Mercy"
Mark 10:46-52

Then they came to Jericho. And as He was leaving Jericho with His disciples and a large crowd, a blind beggar named Bartimaeus, the son of Timaeus, was sitting by the road. ⁴⁷ When he heard that it was Jesus the Nazarene, he began to cry out and say, "Jesus, Son of David, have mercy on me!" ⁴⁸ Many were sternly telling him to be quiet, but he kept crying out all the more, "Son of David, have mercy on me!" ⁴⁹ And Jesus stopped and said, "Call him here." So they *called the blind man, saying to him, "Take courage, stand up! He is calling for you." ⁵⁰ Throwing aside his cloak, he jumped up and came to Jesus. ⁵¹ And answering him, Jesus said, "What do you want Me to do for you?" And the blind man said to Him, "Rabboni, I want to regain my sight!" ⁵² And Jesus said to him, "Go; your faith has made you well." Immediately he regained his sight and began following Him on the road.

INTRODUCTION

BARTIMAEUS WAS A MAN WHO could easily be lost in a crowd. He was blind. He was a beggar. He was dependent on others. He was a discarded member of society for the most part. Yet, in him we see an attitude that would not give up.

Bartimaeus reminds me of the illustration of the hummingbird and the vulture. Both of these birds fly over the desert of the Southwest United States. All vultures look for is rotting dead flesh that they can feast upon. Hummingbirds, on the other hand, ignore the dead rotting flesh and look instead for colorful desert plant blooms. Vultures live on what once was. They fill up on what is past, dead and gone. But hummingbirds live on what is. They seek to fill up on what is living and healthy. Each of these birds finds exactly what they are looking for.

When Bartimaeus heard Jesus was near he cried out for mercy. "Jesus, Son of David, have mercy on me!" Mercy is undeserved favor, kindness or compassion given to you by someone else that you didn't deserve.

Bartimaeus' cry for mercy was an acknowledgement of his deplorable condition of misery, unworthiness and helplessness. He was fully dependent on others for his sustenance. That is why he was begging outside the city of Jericho when Jesus passed by.

We can learn a lot about our attitude from blind Bartimaeus.

He Had a PERSISTENT Attitude

He didn't let his blindness hinder him from living life and he didn't let his lot in life as a beggar hinder him (verse 46). He didn't let other people keep him quiet (verse 48). He had a desperate need that made him persistent.

He Had a PROMPT Attitude

He was called over by Jesus because of his persistence. He began crying out all the more when he found out it was Jesus, "Have mercy on me!" (verse 48). Jesus was on His way to Jerusalem but He stopped and called for Bartimaeus to come to Him. Bartimaeus jumped up, threw off his cloak, and ran to Jesus (verse 50). The reproofs of the crowd changed to encouragement when Jesus called for Bartimaeus (verse 49).

He Had a PRECISE Attitude

Bartimaeus knew what he wanted. Jesus asked him, "What do you want Me to do for you?" You would think that it was obvious what a blind man wanted. Jesus asks the question to help the man develop his faith.

It gave the man the chance to express his faith and explain what mercy he was looking for. Bartimaeus was precise about his request. He said in verse 51, "I want to regain my sight!"

He Had a PRECIOUS Attitude

Bartimaeus is the only person other than Mary (John 20:16) to call Jesus "Rabboni," which means, "My dear respected Master" or "My Lord" which was a term of very personal faith. "Son of David", which Bartimaeus uses twice, was a national Jewish messianic term. But Bartimaeus saw Jesus as more than that. He saw Him as his personal Messiah.

Bartimaeus began by begging for alms but he found something more precious than silver or gold. He found the Savior! Matthew's account of this says there were two blind men begging by the road. Mark and Luke just tell us about Bartimaeus. Matthew says Jesus was moved with compassion, touched their eyes and immediately they could see. Mark and Luke don't include Jesus touching the eyes.

CONCLUSION

This blind Bartimaeus had faith. Jesus tells him in verse 52, "Go your way; your faith has made you well." The NASV footnotes if as, "Go your way; your faith has saved you."

This blind man immediately received his sight and began following Jesus on the road. There would be no more begging on the road. He now was walking the same road Jesus was walking.

Maybe you feel like your circumstances or your health or your age or something else has forced you to the side of the road. Don't let the crowd, your needs or your situation stop you from having an attitude that takes you to Jesus. He is all you need. Come to Jesus. Jump up as Bartimaeus did and come to Jesus! Throw off the cloak of whatever is stopping you from coming to Jesus! He wants to give you mercy and become your Lord and Savior.

Discussion Questions

1. What did Bartimaeus cry out when he heard Jesus was near?

2. What made Bartimaeus so persistent?

3. Why do you think Jesus had Bartimaeus come to Him?

4. Why did Jesus ask the blind man what he wanted?

5. What does "Rabboni" mean?

6. What did Bartimaeus see Jesus as?

7. What did Bartimaeus do after Jesus gave him his sight?

Chapter 31

"The Lord Has Need of It"
Mark 11:1-11

As they approached Jerusalem, at Bethphage and Bethany, near the Mount of Olives, He sent two of His disciples, ² and said to them, "Go into the village opposite you, and immediately as you enter it, you will find a colt tied there, on which no one yet has ever sat; untie it and bring it here. ³ If anyone says to you, 'Why are you doing this?' you say, 'The Lord has need of it'; and immediately he will send it back here." ⁴ They went away and found a colt tied at the door, outside in the street; and they untied it. ⁵ Some of the bystanders were saying to them, "What are you doing, untying the colt?" ⁶ They spoke to them just as Jesus had told them, and they gave them permission. ⁷ They brought the colt to Jesus and put their coats on it; and He sat on it. ⁸ And many spread their coats in the road, and others spread leafy branches which they had cut from the fields. ⁹ Those who went in front and those who followed were shouting: "Hosanna! BLESSED IS HE WHO COMES IN THE NAME OF THE LORD; ¹⁰ Blessed is the coming kingdom of our father David; Hosanna in the highest!"

INTRODUCTION

THIS MESSAGE IS ABOUT THE "Triumphal Entry" of Jesus into Jerusalem. It was Passover, the yearly feast to remember the miraculous deliverance of the Jews from Egyptian slavery. All adult males were to come to Jerusalem for the Passover if possible. The Passover tripled the population of Jerusalem, some say to almost a million.

The increase of people put the Roman army on alert as they feared a riot caused by Zealots or some other religious group. Jesus came into Jerusalem when tensions were high. Jesus took the road from Bethany to Jerusalem which was about two miles. There was a spectacular view of Jerusalem as you walked these two miles from the east to the west.

Jesus was on a mission. In one week He would be arrested, crucified, buried and resurrected. This text is upbeat and positive. It would be refreshing if we didn't know what was going to happen in the next few days of Jesus' life.

The Lord Has Need of the Colt

Jesus sent two disciples to fetch the colt of a donkey that had never been sat upon. They would find it tied up and waiting. If anyone questioned their taking the colt they were to say, "The Lord has need of it." This is exactly what happened. They took the colt back to Jesus and He sat upon it after they put some of their garments on it as a makeshift saddle. Jesus riding on the colt fulfilled the prophecy of Zechariah 9:9. This fulfillment showed that Jesus was the Messiah and challenged the religious leaders. This challenge started in motion the plot that within a week would see Jesus crucified and on the cross.

We don't know if Jesus had prearranged with the colt's owner to use the colt or not. But when Jesus had need of it the man allowed it to be used. What do we have that Jesus wants to use? When He needs it are we willing to allow him to use it? When he needs to use us are we willing to be used?

The Lord Has Need of Our Garments

It was customary for citizens to take off their outer garments and lay them in the road along with tree branches when a king approached. This was a way of honoring and praising the king. They cried "Hosanna" which means "save us now!" They recognized Jesus as the son of David and the One who came in the name of the Lord. Mark doesn't mention it because he wrote mainly to Gentiles, but Luke's account (Luke 19:39, 40) tells us that the Jewish religious leaders tried to get Jesus to make the people stop crying out their praises. But Jesus says that if the people stop praising Him then the rocks will have to cry out.

The people's praises were a fulfillment of prophecy (Psalm 118:22, 23). What praises do we have to pour out on our Lord? How are we honoring our Savior and King? If Jesus was riding down our street, what would we do?

The Lord Has Need of Our Recognition of Him

Jesus came into Jerusalem as a triumphant king but He was not the kind of king most of the people were hoping for. He was king of the Jews but He did not come to establish an earthly kingdom. The Romans were experts with parades. We call this incident in Jesus' final week the "Triumphal Entry" but it wasn't much like a "Roman Triumph." Before a Roman General could have a triumphal entry through Rome he had to have killed 5,000 enemy in his conquests. Then he was given an elaborate official parade. This parade consisted of a ride in a golden chariot through the streets with priests burning incense in his honor. Important captured enemies were bound and lead in a procession along with spoils and other treasures that had been captured. The procession would often end in the Roman Coliseum where the captured prisoners would be thrown to the wild animals. The people would cheer and praise the Roman general for his victory over the enemy.

Jesus came into Jerusalem with nothing more than the colt and a crowd that didn't really know what was happening. The people blessed Him because He came in the name of the Lord. He was bringing a spiritual kingdom which they knew nothing about. But it wouldn't be long before there would be well over 5,000 who died to their sins and named Jesus as their Lord. The death, burial and resurrection of Jesus would turn the world upside down (Acts 17:6) before too much longer.

We need to see Jesus Christ as the King of Kings and Lord of Lords. We need to recognize Him for who He really is. The Lord has need of us to recognize Him as Lord and Savior. Is that who He is to you?

CONCLUSION

F.J. Tomkinson wrote:

THE LORD HAS NEED OF IT

Peter had a boat to save Him from the press;
Martha lent her home with busy kindliness.
One man lent a colt, another lent an upper room;
Some threw down their clothes, and Joseph lent a tomb.
Simon lent his strength the cruel cross to bear;
Mary her spices brought, His body to prepare.
What have I to lend - no boat, no house, no lands;
Dwell, Lord, in my heart and use my feeble hands.

Jesus' triumphal entry into your life could begin today if you would accept Him as your personal Savior. If you have already done that then He wants you to continue living a life of praise to Him because the Lord has need of you!

Discussion Questions

1. What did the Passover do to the city of Jerusalem?

2. What were the two disciples to say if anyone questioned them about taking the donkey?

3. What does" Hosanna" mean?

4. What would happen if we don't praise the Lord?

5. Explain what a Roman Triumph is?

6. When did the Triumphal Entry take place in Jesus' ministry?

7. What kind of a kingdom did Jesus come to establish, and what did the death, burial and resurrection accomplish?

Chapter 32

"The Rejected Stone"
Mark 12:1-12

And He began to speak to them in parables: "A man PLANTED A VINEYARD AND PUT A WALL AROUND IT, AND DUG A VAT UNDER THE WINE PRESS AND BUILT A TOWER, *and rented it out to vine-growers and went on a journey.* [2] *At the harvest time he sent a slave to the vine-growers, in order to receive some of the produce of the vineyard from the vine-growers.* [3] *They took him, and beat him and sent him away empty-handed* [4] *Again he sent them another slave, and they wounded him in the head, and treated him shamefully.* [5] *And he sent another, and that one they killed; and so with many others, beating some and killing others.* [6] *He had one more to send, a beloved son; he sent him last of all to them, saying, 'They will respect my son.'* [7] *But those vine-growers said to one another, 'This is the heir; come, let us kill him, and the inheritance will be ours!'* [8] *They took him, and killed him and threw him out of the vineyard.* [9] *What will the owner of the vineyard do? He will come and destroy the vine-growers, and will give the vineyard to others.* [10] *Have you not even read this Scripture:*

'THE STONE WHICH THE BUILDERS REJECTED, THIS BECAME THE CHIEF CORNER *stone;*[11] THIS CAME ABOUT FROM THE LORD, AND IT IS MARVELOUS IN OUR EYES'.*"*

¹² And they were seeking to seize Him, and yet they feared the people, for they understood that He spoke the parable against them. And so they left Him and went away.

INTRODUCTION

I FOUND OUT SOMETHING AMAZING ABOUT the West Goshen Cemetery recently. Most of you know where the cemetery is just east of our church building on the south side of Berkey Ave. It seems that the cemetery, which is overseen by the city of Goshen, has a rule on the books that people living on the north side of Berkey Ave. cannot be buried in the cemetery. Yeah, it seemed like a stupid rule to me, too. But you see, they have a strict policy about burying people that are still alive!

In our text today, the religious leaders were trying to trip Jesus up with trick questions. Jesus saw through their trick questions and told a parable that was designed to reveal where their sins were leading them. The religious leaders' lack of obedience to God was leading them away from the truth. They were not seeking what was true or right but what was safe. This parable is about authority and ownership. This parable asks the question, "What will we do with Jesus?"

According to Lev. 19, a farmer would not use grapes from the vineyard until the 5th year. The vines still had to be tended and other crops could be grown in between the growing rows of vines. Verse 1 tells us that the owner rents out the vineyard to tenant farmers during the first years when the grapes were not used. Lev. 19 tells us that the fourth year, when harvest time came, the grapes were harvested but they were given to the Lord. In the fifth year the farmer could then start harvesting the grapes for himself.

The first three years the owner sent slaves to receive some of the produce that was rightfully his. In order to keep legal claim to the land the owner had to receive some produce from the tenant farmers who were renting his land. The renters believed that if they could avoid paying anything to the owner they would eventually get the property for themselves.

The slaves that are sent but not accepted represent the prophets that God sent to Israel. The message the prophets told was rejected. Jesus was saying to the religious leaders that they had rejected the prophets God had sent and even had killed some of them.

It is more than coincidence that the owner sends his own beloved son in the fourth year. Verse 6 says that he thought they would respect his son. But the renters figured that if they killed the son, who was the only heir, they would get the vineyard for themselves. Wrong!

Jesus asks, "What will the owner of the vineyard do?" The answer is obvious. He will destroy the vineyard renters and give the vineyard to others. Here Jesus was stating the obvious that since the Jews rejected Him, He would give the kingdom to the Gentiles.

Jesus quotes a Messianic prophecy from Psalm 118 that the religious leaders would have known. He says "The Stone" (which was a well-known term describing the Messiah) would be rejected.

The Jewish religious leaders and most of the Jews had rejected "The Son" and "The Stone." The owner, who was God, sent His Son. The Son was not only rejected, but they crucified Him! The Jewish leaders thought it was over but 3 days later He came back to life.

Although the Jewish leaders wanted to seize Jesus they couldn't because of the multitude. They knew Jesus was speaking about them. But all they could do for now was walk away. But they would be back.

This parable tells us a lot about God. He is generous and had a well-equipped vineyard. He is trustable and lets others take care of what he owns. He is patient and gives us many chances to do what is right. Yet, He is a just Judge and gives out judgment that is true.

We learn in this parable that Christ was more than a messenger and a servant. He was the Son and the promised Messiah. He was "The Stone" that was to become the chief cornerstone that the builders rejected.

We learn about ourselves that we think we can get away with anything. But God knows and sees all. What we have can be taken away from us and it can be given to others. We also learn that there will be a day coming when we will have to give an account for how we have lived and the kind of stewardship that we practiced during our life on the earth.

CONCLUSION

What will we do with Jesus? Will we build our lives upon the Rock, the Chief Cornerstone? Will we build upon the Rock that doesn't roll? Unless we receive the Son, "The Stone", we will be the ones that are rejected because we never really knew the Lord.

Why not make today harvest time! Give the Lord authority and ownership of your life. You will not be disappointed if you do.

Discussion Questions

1. How were the religious leaders trying to trip up Jesus?

2. What is this parable about?

3. What question is this parable asking us?

4. Tell how a farmer cares for grape vines?

5. What did the slaves sent to collect produce from the renters represent?

6. The owner's own son was sent the fourth year, but what happened to him and who did he represent?

7. Why was the son, Jesus, called "The Stone"?

Chapter 33

"The Money Trap"
Mark 12:13-17

Then they sent some of the Pharisees and Herodians to Him in order to trap Him in a statement. [14] They came and said to Him, "Teacher, we know that You are truthful and defer to no one; for You are not partial to any, but teach the way of God in truth. Is it lawful to pay a poll-tax to Caesar, or not? [15] Shall we pay or shall we not pay?" But He, knowing their hypocrisy, said to them, "Why are you testing Me? Bring Me a denarius to look at." [16] They brought one. And He said to them, "Whose likeness and inscription is this?" And they said to Him, "Caesar's." [17] And Jesus said to them, "Render to Caesar the things that are Caesar's, and to God the things that are God's." And they were amazed at Him.

INTRODUCTION

A MAN ON VACATION WAS STROLLING along outside his hotel in Acapulco, enjoying the sunny Mexican weather. Suddenly, his walk was interrupted by the screams of a woman kneeling in front of a child. The man knew enough Spanish to determine that the child had swallowed a coin. Seizing the child by the heels, the man held him up, gave him a few shakes, and an American quarter dropped to the sidewalk. "Oh, thank you, sir!" cried the woman. "You seemed to know just how to get it out of him. Are you a doctor?" "No, ma'am," replied the man. "I'm with the United States Internal Revenue Service." *Bits & Pieces*, March 31, 1994, p. 5.

In Luke's account of the birth of Christ, he tells us that Caesar Augustus decreed that a censes should be taken which meant every person had to return to the city of their birth to be enrolled in the census. There were two reasons for the census. One was so the Romans could find new prospects for their army. The other reason was so they could make everyone pay a tax.

The Romans controlled Judea and required the people to pay three taxes:

1) A ground tax. 1/10 of all grain and 1/5 of all wine and fruit.
2) An income tax of 1% of all income.
3) A poll tax on all men 14-65 and women 12-65 (about 1 denarius per person equal to approximately $15 US.)

The paying of taxes was a political hot spot and the Jewish leaders thought it might be an area where they could trap Jesus.

SETTING THE TRAP

The scribes, chief priests and Jewish elders were getting desperate to find a plot that would work to catch Jesus (Mark 11:27). They sent some Pharisees and Herodians to try to trap Jesus with a question about taxes. We know the Jewish leaders were desperate because the Pharisees and Herodians didn't get along and they didn't believe the same things. The Herodians supported the family of Herod and the Romans. The Pharisees hated the Herodians because they thought Herod had usurped David's throne and he was not a Jew. The Pharisees didn't like the Romans or their taxes.

The Herodians and Pharisees hoped to catch Jesus saying something that they could use against Him (vs 13). Their trap was a question: "Is it lawful to pay a poll tax to Caesar or not?" (vs 14). They thought they had Him because if He said it was OK to pay tribute to Caesar He would lose all His followers and if He said it was not lawful to pay the tax then they could arrest Jesus as a traitor. They thought they had Jesus caught in their trap no matter how He answered.

STEALING OF THE BAIT

Jesus knew they were setting a trap for Him. He knew their hypocrisy. "Shall we pay or shall we not pay a poll tax to Caesar? That was the question. That was the bait to catch Jesus (vs 14, 15). Jesus asks them to bring Him a denarius coin. A denarius was the equivalent to a day's wage.

Jesus looked at the coin for a while and then He asks them whose picture was on the coin (vs 16). Caesar's picture was on the coin. The reverse side of the coin had words hailing Caesar as the religious leader. Caesar had used his authority to create the coins. All who used the coins with his image on them accepted Caesar's authority and believed the coins had value.

Jesus took the coin and made an object lesson out of it. What He did was steal their bait from their own trap and He used it against them.

When I was a teenager I trapped muskrats to make some money. I had one trap that was in a great looking spot with signs of fresh activity. I set the trap and was pretty confident I would catch a muskrat the next day when I ran my trap line. Sure enough, the next day I caught something. I followed the chain to the trap and had a muskrat foot. I had caught one but he chewed off his foot and got away. I reset the trap in the same spot. The next day I caught another foot. The third day the same thing happened. On the forth I caught a foot also, but this time the rest of the muskrat was attached. When I pulled the drowned muskrat out of the water he had three feet missing! He had avoided getting caught three times.

SPRINGING THE TRAP

Because Jesus knew they were setting the trap for Him he was able to turn their trap on them. When I was trapping, my hands would get so cold I could hardly feel anything. There was nothing worse than having the trap snap shut on your cold hands. Jesus was going to snap the trap shut on the Herodians and the Pharisees. He would also catch the chief priests, scribes and Jewish leaders who had sent them to trap Him.

Jesus responded to their question of paying taxes with this statement: "Render to Caesar the things that are Caesar's, and to God the things that are God's" (verse 17). "Render" means to pay a debt or to pay back what you owe. Jesus affirmed that citizens have a debt to the government for services rendered. Christians may not always like the way the government uses our tax money but we still have an obligation to pay the debt we owe because the government is established by God (Romans 13).

Jesus also said that we have a debt to God and we should "render" to God the things that are God's. What do you suppose would happen if we paid taxes like we give to the church?

Jesus had taken the trap that the Herodians and Pharisees had set to catch Him and He turned it on them and caught them in their own trap. Verse 17 says that "they were amazed at Him."

CONCLUSION

The coin that was used in this trap was a sign of power. When someone became a ruler, he would issue coins with his likeness on them. This ruler or king was viewed as having power wherever his coins were accepted as legal tender. The coin Jesus asked for belonged to Caesar because it had his image and name on it. The things of God have His image and name on them. Do you bear the name or image of God? Does the Lord have power over your life?

Discussion Questions

1. In Jesus' day, what taxes did the Romans require people to pay?

2. How do we know that the Jewish leaders are desperate to trap Jesus?

3. What question did the Jewish leaders ask in hopes of trapping Jesus?

4. What is the value of a denarius coin?

5. How did Jesus answer the question of paying taxes to Caesar?

6. What does the word "render" mean?

7. What did the people think about Jesus' answer?

Chapter 34

"The Most Important Commandment"
Mark 12:28-34

One of the scribes came and heard them arguing, and recognizing that He had answered them well, asked Him, "What commandment is the foremost of all?" 29 Jesus answered, "The foremost is, 'Hear, O Israel! The Lord our God is one Lord; 30 and you shall love the Lord your God with all your heart, and with all your soul, and with all your mind, and with all your strength.' 31 The second is this, 'You shall love your neighbor as yourself.' There is no other commandment greater than these." 32 The scribe said to Him, "Right, Teacher; You have truly stated that He is One, and there is no one else besides Him; 33 and to love Him with all the heart and with all the understanding and with all the strength, and to love one's neighbor as himself, is much more than all burnt offerings and sacrifices." 34 When Jesus saw that he had answered intelligently, He said to him, "You are not far from the kingdom of God." After that, no one would venture to ask Him any more questions.

INTRODUCTION

OUR DESIRE AS CHRISTIANS IS to do the will of God isn't it? If we love God we will keep His commandments (1 John 2:2). Of all the things God has communicated to us in the Bible, what do you think He would put at the top of His list for us to do? That is the question that is asked in this text.

According to Warren Wiersbe, the scribes had determined that there were 613 commands in the law given to Moses that the Jews were bound to obey. Three hundred sixty-five commands were negative and 248 were positive.

The scribe that came to Jesus does not seem to be trying to trick Jesus. He seems sincere about wanting to know which commandment was the most important. He asks, "What commandment is the foremost of all?" (NASV) The NIV, Living and Good News say, "What commandment is the most important?" and the KJV says, "Which commandment is the greatest?" This question is about priorities. Let's look at what Jesus said was the most important commandment.

The Challenge of the Most Important Commandment

There is only one God that we are to love. There is no one else besides Him (verse 32). This is important because we cannot serve two masters (Mt. 6:24). We must be totally surrendered to the Lord. There is always trouble when we divide our allegiance.

We are to love the Lord with all our heart, soul, mind and strength. Some would split these four ways we are to love God. That can be done, but the meaning here is that we are to love God with our total being. Mark's point was not to show differing aspects of how we love God but to show that our love is to be complete. Jesus made our loving God the most important thing in life that we can do.

The Companion of the Most Important Commandment

Even though the scribe only asked Jesus for the most important commandment Jesus gave him a second commandment that was a companion to the first and could not be separated from it easily. Keeping the first commandment leads to the second commandment. We are to love our neighbor as our self.

We cannot say we love God and hate our neighbor (1 John 4:20,21). These two commandments go together. These two commands were part of the Shema (morning and evening prayer, said by all Jews). The scribe acknowledged that Jesus had answered correctly (verse 32).

If we really love God then we will automatically love others. A loving relationship to God enables us to love the people that God loves. Our living is not about keeping rules but about relationships. If we are in a right relationship with God then we will want to do what He says.

The Conviction of the Most Important Commandment

This scribe was convicted by Jesus' answer as he intelligently considered it and admitted that loving God and loving other people was much more important than offering burnt offerings and sacrifices (verse 33). This scribe who had at one time sided with the Pharisees and others who were after evidence against Jesus, now was declaring Jesus to be right.

Having an understanding of this most important commandment brings you close to being a part of the kingdom of God. Jesus told the scribe, "You are not far from the kingdom of God." Jesus gave this scribe the opportunity to continue seeking the kingdom of God. We are not told whether this scribe followed up on his conviction and made it into the kingdom of God. This scribe, like any of us, had the opportunity to consider the truth and then decide upon it. I would like to think that this scribe did decide to be a part of the kingdom. Jesus' answer (a quotation of the OT law) and the conviction of this scribe were too much for those seeking to trap Jesus. Verse 34 says that no one else would ask Jesus a question after that.

CONCLUSION

Knowing what the most important commandment is and obeying it is not the same thing. It is easy to know the most important commandment. It is hard to love God and others. But knowing the most important commandment is a good start to keeping it.

I don't think we can really keep this commandment on our own. Without

Jesus Christ as our Lord and Savior, it will be difficult. But if Jesus Christ is our Lord and Savior we will have help to love God and love others.

Discussion Questions

1. How many commandments did Moses give the people?

2. What is the greatest commandment?

3. What commandment goes with the most important commandment?

4. Understanding the greatest commandment does what for you?

5. Did the Scribe make it into the kingdom?

6. What is the hardest part about the greatest commandment?

7. What can you do to keep this greatest commandment?

Chapter 35

"Surplus or Sacrificial Giving?"
Mark 12:41-44

And He sat down opposite the treasury, and began observing how the people were putting money into the treasury; and many rich people were putting in large sums. [42] A poor widow came and put in two small copper coins, which amount to a cent. [43] Calling His disciples to Him, He said to them, "Truly I say to you, this poor widow put in more than all the contributors to the treasury [44] for they all put in out of their surplus, but she, out of her poverty, put in all she owned, all she had to live on."

INTRODUCTION

WITH JUST THREE DAYS LEFT before Jesus went to the cross He was concerned about how people worship. Specifically, He was interested in how they gave offerings to God.

A little boy was given two quarters as he was sent off to church about 3 blocks away. His dad told him that he should put one quarter in the offering and on the way home from church he could spend the other one on gum or candy. He was playing with the quarters as he was walking to church and he dropped one of the quarters and before he could catch up to it, it rolled into the drain gutter along the curb. He looked at the remaining quarter in his hand and said to himself, "Well, God, there goes your offering down the drain!"

Remember, Mark's version of the Gospel is more like Reader's Digest than an encyclopedia. Mark was more interested in what Jesus did than what He said. Mark's Gospel is about action. In this text Mark tells us of Jesus sitting near the temple observing people as they were giving their offering. Let's look at what Jesus said about "Surplus or Sacrificial Giving".

The Setting

Jesus may have been teaching in the temple. Jesus had finished His discussion and went to set down at the gate called "Beautiful" that was within sight of the Court of Women where the offerings were collected.

In the Court of Women there were 13 treasure chest type boxes that had trumpet looking tubes coming out of them at various locations around the walls. These boxes were labeled for different purposes. Oil for lamps, wood for altar, sacrificial animals, temple tribute, incense, money for the poor, temple upkeep etc. People could give to whatever they wanted by dropping their coins into the proper trumpet.

Jesus saw people dropping in their offerings. He noticed the rich putting in large offerings. He also saw a widow put in two small copper coins that were worth about half a penny. The rich made a big show out of giving so that people noticed (Matthew 6:1-4). The widow, however, gave humbly and was hardly noticed.

Jesus was not impressed by the gifts of the rich even though they were large. What impressed Jesus was the gift of the widow. Even though it was very small, it was all that she had. It was a real sacrifice, while the rich gifts were out of their surplus. The widow could have kept one coin for herself and given the other one to God but she gave them both. By giving all she had she shows her faith and dependence on God to take care of her. Jesus was so impressed with what He saw, He called the disciples over to teach them an important lesson.

The Lesson

Jesus only called the 12 together when He wanted them to learn something important from Him. The idea is that of summoning someone to come to you because you have something important to say and you don't want them to miss it. Jesus does this with the disciples in Mark 3:13, 6:7, 8:1 and 34, 10:42 and here in 12:43.

Jesus pointed out what real worship in giving was by showing the disciples this widow who gave sacrificially all she had. The rich people were only giving out of their surplus. Jesus wanted them to see the contrast in these two attitudes of giving. Jesus had the ability to see beyond the amount into the heart of the giver. We need to understand that He sees into our hearts too, when we give. Jesus measured the gift, not by the amount given, but by the amount that was left after the gift was given.

True giving that pleases the Lord is sacrificially given. It is not the amount of the gift but the cost of the gift that matters. David declared that he would not offer a sacrifice to God that cost him nothing (2 Sam. 24:24). Although our Lord notices the size of the gift, what impresses Him is the sacrifice that we make to give our gift.

When was the last time you sacrificed so you could give something to God? When was the last time it hurt to give your gift? Jesus told the disciples that the rich gave out of their surplus but the widow gave sacrificially out of her poverty.

1 Timothy 6:10 says- "For the love of money is a root of all sorts of evil, and some by longing for it have wandered away from the faith, and pierced themselves with many a pang."

A badger met a skunk one day
Who would not share the right of way
And raised his battle flag and said,
"If you want trouble just come ahead."
The badger said, "You little squirt
You are a stinker – mean as dirt.
But since you have so much B. O.
I will step aside and let you go."
The moral of this episode
Can serve you well along life's road
Stay clear from all that would defile
Though it makes you walk an extra mile.
-anonymous from the Lamplighter, Las Vegas, NV

CONCLUSION

It may be scary to depend upon God for your daily bread. But God blesses givers who give sacrificially. You can never out give God. When God sees your gift is He pleased or embarrassed? I can almost see the Lord sitting up in heaven watching our giving. How many of us give in such a way that the Lord would be impressed and summon the disciples or the angels over and say, "Look at what that child of mine gave today!"

Probably nothing we do expresses our love relationship with the Lord more than our giving. I don't know what anyone gives in our offering - but God does.

Mark thought that this incident was important to include in His Gospel. I think the disciples got the lesson Jesus wanted them to learn. They gave everything in service to Him, including their lives.

I don't expect this lesson will make anyone sell all they have and give the money away to the poor. But maybe, just maybe, some of you will re-evaluate your attitude of giving and start giving more sacrificially instead of out of your surplus.

This was certainly one of the important last lessons Jesus taught us before He went to the cross.

Discussion Questions

1. How does the timing of this lesson on giving stress its importance?

2. Where did this lesson take place?

3. How much did the widow put in the offering and what was significant about her gift?

4. What did Jesus point out about relationships in giving?

5. Jesus has the ability to see beyond the amount of our gift to what?

6. What is true giving that pleases the Lord?

7. What expresses our love for the Lord more than anything else?

Chapter 36

"Be on the Alert"
Mark 13:14-37

INTRODUCTION

WITH THIS STUDY WE COME to the close of Mark's Gospel except for the final week narratives of Jesus' life. We will have three more studies from Mark. The last topic Mark writes about before he moves into the final week material is concerning the second coming.

Mark emphasizes the importance of our being on the alert by repeating the idea 4 times in verses 33-37.

1. Verse 33- keep on the alert
2. Verse 34- stay on the alert
3. Verse 35- be on the alert
4. Verse 37- be on the alert

An older congregation was having trouble finding a minister so they decided to try for a weekend student minister in hopes that it would become full time upon his graduation from Bible College. The student that came to the church had very little experience preaching but was willing to do his best. The first Sunday he started out pretty good until he forgot what came next. His preaching professor had told the class that if you forget what comes next go back and repeat what you just said and maybe it will come to you. The last thing he had said was "Behold, I come quickly." So he repeated it. "Behold, I come quickly." But nothing came to him. So he said it one more time and smacked the pulpit thinking that might help. When he said, "Behold I come quickly" the third time and smacked the pulpit, the pulpit gave way and he landed right in the lap of a 90 year old lady in the front row. He was embarrassed and apologized over and over but the little old lady said, "No need to apologize. You warned me three times you were coming!"

In this study we want to look at Mark's emphasis on being ready for the Lord's return whenever it may come.

"Because There is No Time for Planning" – verses 14-18

You can't really plan for when Jesus will return. You should not wait till he comes to get ready. There will be no time to get down off the roof. There will be no time to go back to the house to get a coat. There will be no time to have a baby. Winter is a bad time for Jesus to return because it is a slower process then. This all was to emphasize the need for urgency at being on the alert.

"Because It Will Be a Time of Tribulation" – verses 19,20

Tribulation means troubles, stress, oppression and pain that comes from an outside source that can be physical, mental or spiritual in nature. It is usually thought of as a period of time near the return of Christ. This tribulation will be worse than any man has ever known. Jesus was probably talking about the destruction of Jerusalem that was coming soon. But He also could be referring to past events in history or even future events to come when Jesus returns.

"Because It Is a Time of Many False Prophets" – (verses 21-23

There will be many who claim to be Christ or a prophet. They will be able to do signs and wonders which will be used to trick people and try to lead people away from the truth. This is a good description of the way cults work. The "elect" refers to the church, the chosen ones, Christians. If we stand firm upon the truth it won't be possible to be lead astray.

"Because Once Jesus Comes It's Too Late" – verses 24-37

Jesus illustrates the Second Coming in three ways:
1. (verses 24-27) a picture from Matthew 24 and Revelation. Read these verses. This picture is of desperate times and situations describing the coming of Jesus and the gathering of the saints.
2. (verses 28-32) this second illustration is the parable of the fig tree. This parable is different from another that Jesus told. Here the point is that when a fig tree gets its leaves summer is near. When the things in verses 24-27 start happening you can know that Jesus' return is near. He is right at the door! Jesus makes the bold statement that even though you can tell when His return might be near no one but the Father knows the exact day and time. Jesus doesn't even know. It seems that Jesus is speaking about two things here. His own return and also the tribulation and destruction of Jerusalem that would happen in these peoples lifetime.
3. (verses 33-37) is the third illustration of a man on a journey. The master of the house goes away leaving servants in charge of various duties. They don't know when the master will be back. He probably didn't tell them because he didn't know for sure. But he would be back. If the servants goofed off and did not do their assigned duties they could be put to death. Since they do not know when the master is coming back they needed to stay busy and not go to sleep on their jobs. There was work to be done and also protection to be maintained by the doorkeeper.

CONCLUSION

This message of being alert was being said to "all" (verse 37). There was urgency in the way Mark ends his Gospel. Verse 5- "see to it that no one misleads you." Verse 13- "be on guard so that you endure to the end so that you may be saved." Verse 33- "Keep on the alert." Verse 34- "Stay on the alert." Verse 35- "Be on the alert." Verse 37- "Be on the alert."

In other words be ready, be watching, and stay awake!

Are you ready? The time is now! The day is today! Jesus may come and what will you say?

Discussion Questions

1. How does Mark emphasize the need to be ready for Jesus' return?

2. Why is it so important to be ready when Jesus comes?

3. What tribulation was Jesus probably talking about in verses 19 and 20?

4. Who will make it difficult in the last days to stay faithful to the Lord?

5. How did Mark illustrate that when Jesus comes again it will be too late?

6. How does Mark show a sense of urgency about Jesus coming again?

7. What can you do to be ready for the Lord's return?

Chapter 37

"In Memory of Her"
Mark 14:3-9

While He was in Bethany at the home of Simon the leper, and reclining at the table, there came a woman with an alabaster vial of very costly perfume of pure nard; and she broke the vial and poured it over His head. ⁴But some were indignantly remarking to one another, "Why has this perfume been wasted? ⁵ For this perfume might have been sold for over three hundred denarii, and the money given to the poor." And they were scolding her. ⁶ But Jesus said, "Let her alone; why do you bother her? She has done a good deed to Me. ⁷ For you always have the poor with you, and whenever you wish you can do good to them; but you do not always have Me. ⁸ She has done what she could; she has anointed My body beforehand for the burial. ⁹ Truly I say to you, wherever the gospel is preached in the whole world, what this woman has done will also be spoken of in memory of her."

INTRODUCTION

JESUS WAS IN THE HOME of Simon the leper, who lived in Bethany just outside Jerusalem, but we shouldn't call him a leper anymore because he had been healed by Jesus. Simon's guests and Jesus were reclined at a table to eat.

A woman with an expensive alabaster vial of perfume anointed Jesus in an expression of deep love for Him by breaking the vial and pouring it on Jesus' head. Mark does not mention the woman's name. In John's account, (John 12:1-8), he tells us that this woman is Mary, sister of Martha and Lazarus.

In the Gospels we find Mary mentioned three times - here, in John 11 (where Lazarus is raised), and in Luke 10:38-42 (where her sister Martha is upset with her for not helping fix the meal when Jesus visited their home). All three times we find Mary at the feet of Jesus. Let's take a closer look at Mary's anointing of Jesus.

"She Has Done a Good Deed" – verse 6

The alabaster vial was not expensive. It was just the pottery container that held the expensive pure nard. Nard was an ointment like perfume that was made from the root of the spikenard plant. It came from northern India and cost the average person a year's wage. John says it was a pound of nard. Breaking the vial was symbolic of death. As bodies were prepared for burial the broken pottery was left in a pile to symbolize a body broken by death.

Mary poured the costly perfume over Jesus' head (verse 3) and John adds that Mary also poured it on Jesus' feet and used her hair to wipe it off (John 12:3). Some thought that it was a waste for Mary to do this. They scolded her because the nard was worth over 300 danarii which was equivalent to almost a full year of wages which could have been given to the poor. True love does not count the cost.

Jesus came to Mary's defense. He told the complainers to leave her alone because she had done a good thing. He said the poor are always with you and you can help them anytime. But He wouldn't always be with them (verses 4-7).

"She Did What She Could" - verse 8

The significance of what Mary did, although she may not have known it, was that her anointing of Jesus was actually preparing Him for His death that would come in less than a week on the cross. Jesus may have known that his death would happen so that there would not be adequate time to prepare His body after He died.

Mary couldn't do a lot of things. But she could be near Jesus when she had the chance. Mary saw that being near Jesus is important. Jesus reinforced her presence at His feet when He told Martha she was too worried about things and that really there was only one thing that really mattered and that was what Mary had chosen - to be seated at the feet of Jesus learning from Him (Luke 10:38-42).

Mary could have done many things with the expensive nard perfume. But she was willing to give what she had of great value to the Lord. What could you do for Jesus? What can you give Him?

"She Will Be Remembered" - verse 9

Wherever the Gospel is preached in the whole world Mary will be remembered. What she did in anointing Jesus was important and would be credited to her forever. Jesus' approval of what she did was more important than what anyone else thought or said.

Mary did something worth being remembered for. What are you doing that is worth being remembered for? Certainly, what Jesus said about Mary has come true all around the world where the Gospel has gone. People speak of what she did "in memory of her"!

CONCLUSION

Mark tells us that right after this event Judas Iscariot excuses himself and goes out to find the chief priests in order to betray Jesus (Mark 14:10). He may have been the one to speak out about the perfume being wasted. We see quite a contrast between Mary and Judas. They are both remembered, but for what?

How do you want to be remembered? How you will be remembered basically is up to you and how you choose to live your life. It is your choice.

At funerals family members often put things in the coffin that remind them of the person or the life that the person lived. I wonder, if it was you in that coffin, what would people put in there that reminded them of you and your life?

Discussion Questions

1. How do we know that the woman who anointed Jesus was Martha's sister Mary?

2. Where was Mary all three times we see Mary in the Bible?

3. How much was the perfume Mary used to anoint Jesus worth?

4. What do you know about the perfume Mary used to anoint Jesus?

5. What did Mary's anointing of Jesus prepare Him for?

6. Mary did something worth being remembered for. What are you doing that people will remember you for doing?

7. What is different in the way we remember Mary and Judas?

Chapter 38

"Pressed Into Service"
Mark 15:20-27

While He was in Bethany at the home of Simon the leper, and reclining at the table, there came a woman with an alabaster vial of very costly perfume of pure nard; and she broke the vial and poured it over His head. ⁴But some were indignantly remarking to one another, "Why has this perfume been wasted? ⁵For this perfume might have been sold for over three hundred denarii, and the money given to the poor." And they were scolding her. ⁶But Jesus said, "Let her alone; why do you bother her? She has done a good deed to Me. ⁷For you always have the poor with you, and whenever you wish you can do good to them; but you do not always have Me. ⁸ She has done what she could; she has anointed My body beforehand for the burial. ⁹Truly I say to you, wherever the gospel is preached in the whole world, what this woman has done will also be spoken of in memory of her."

INTRODUCTION

W E ARE COMING TO THE end of this Gospel of Mark and our emphasis on serving. But that does not mean that we have to stop looking for ways that we can keep on serving. One of the things the church needs to be known for, is our serving.

This lesson comes from the crucifixion scene in Mark 15. In verse 20 the soldiers have finished mocking Jesus and lead Him out of the city to crucify Him. Jesus has been beaten nearly to death. His body was sleep deprived. His emotions were spent. He was forced to carry the cross piece on which He would be nailed approximately half a mile through the city streets and outside the walls of Jerusalem to Galgotha, called the Place of the Skull, because from a distance it looked like a skull. There, He would be crucified.

In the midst of this tragedy, we are introduced to a man named Simon of Cyrene who is "pressed into service" to help carry Jesus' cross. Let's look at Simon and his service.

Service Sometimes Comes Unexpected

Some might say that Simon was in the wrong place at the wrong time. I say Simon was in the right place at the right time. Sometimes an opportunity to serve comes when we aren't expecting it. Mark 15:21 calls Simon a passerby. Luke 23:26 says He was coming in from the countryside.

Simon was entering the city of Jerusalem just as the soldiers were leading Jesus out of the city to crucify Him. Sometimes we see Jesus in unexpected places. What we do with Him can have eternal consequences.

Service Sometimes is Not Optional

Simon was "pressed" into service. Matthew and Mark both use this word "pressed." Luke says the soldiers "laid hold" of Simon. The word means "to force," "to compel" or "to be pressed" and only appears three times in the New Testament. Twice, in Matthew 27:32 and Mark 15:21, are the accounts of Simon being "pressed into service."

The third time, the word is used by Jesus in Matthew 5:41 – "And whoever shall "force" you to go one mile, go with him two". The Roman soldiers had the right to force you to carry a burden a mile. Jesus says that the way to overcome evil is by doing good. In this case, you would go the extra mile.

Simon was being forced, "pressed into service", and by law he would have had to carry the cross for a mile. But Jesus had already carried the cross half-way to Golgotha. He only had to carry it approximately a quarter of a mile.

Simon didn't have the option of refusing to carry Jesus' cross. He didn't realize it at the time, but carrying the cross of Jesus and serving Him would become the greatest blessing of His life. Sometimes we don't really want to serve but after we have served we realize that it was a special blessing.

Service Sometimes Changes Your Life

Simon was probably a Jew who was in Jerusalem from his home of Cyrene (on the Northern coast of Africa, West of Egypt). There was a large Jewish population there. Simon's service may have been forced, but being near Jesus at some point changed his life as he was converted and became a follower of Christ. Mark tells us that Simon was the father of Alexander and Rufus. Mark mentioned this because they were well known in the early church.

Paul. in writing to the Romans (16:13). sends greetings to Rufus and his mother. Paul even adds the note that he considers Rufus' mother his mother. Evidently the whole family was close to Paul and had been very supportive of his ministry. Simon, being "pressed into service", had an effect upon the whole family. They all seem to be remembered for their service to the Lord.

CONCLUSION

I have no power or authority to "press you into service" for our Lord and Savior Jesus Christ and His church. Serving Jesus has to be your decision. But I hope that our emphasis on serving with love in these lessons has motivated you to want to serve. Serving Jesus is the result of our love for Him. They will know we are Christian's by our love! Jesus' coming again is closer than it ever has been before. There can be no greater hope we could have than for Jesus to find us serving Him and His people when He returns. Will he find you faithfully serving when He returns? He won't force you to serve Him. What is your answer to Him?

Discussion Questions

1. Who was Simon and where was he from?

2. How is it that Simon could be pressed into carrying Jesus' cross?

3. By law, what did you have to do if a Roman soldier asked?

4. Who were Simon's sons?

5. What does Paul tell us about Simon's family?

6. Who has to decide to serve Jesus?

7. Will Jesus find you faithfully serving Him when He returns?

Chapter 39

"Go Preach!"
Mark 16:15,16

And He said to them, "Go into all the world and preach the gospel to all creation. [16] He who has believed and has been baptized shall be saved; but he who has disbelieved shall be condemned."

INTRODUCTION

PROVERBS 11:30 SAYS THAT THE person is wise who wins souls.

This is the last lesson in this series from Mark. This text is Mark's version of the great commission. It is for everyone who is a Christian.

The church today sometimes is more engaged in the great reversal than it is in the great commission. Instead of going and telling we have reversed it to come and hear.

I want you to snap your fingers several times with me. Every time you snapped your fingers, two people died somewhere in the world. In the next 24 hours 176,000 people will die and most of them without Jesus Christ as their Savior.

It is imperative that we penetrate our world. Jesus used illustrations of salt, light, a key, and leaven because they all penetrate. Salt penetrates meat or ice, light penetrates darkness, a key penetrates the lock on a door, and leaven penetrates bread dough. You and I must go and preach.

The word that is translated preach is "kerusso" and it means proclaim aloud, preach, herald, announce, tell or declare. You can't use the excuse that you are not a preacher so you don't have to go. We could say, "Go and tell", "Go and declare" or "Go and announce". Let's look at why we must go preach.

We Must Go Because of the Lost

Jesus came to seek and save the lost (Luke 19:10). Jesus taught us the importance of one lost soul in the parable of the lost sheep (Luke 15:4-7), the parable of the woman who had 10 silver coins but lost one (Luke 15:8-10), and the parable Jesus told about the lost son (Luke 15:22-24).

In each of these examples the point is the same. The importance of finding what is lost. There is nothing more valuable than a soul (Mark 8:36).

We Must Go Because the Lord is Counting on Us

Remember that Mark's gospel is about action. He has told us all the things that Jesus did to help us see the need to go preach. The church was not meant to be a home for us to grow old in. It is a hospital to help the hurting.

You and I are the healers that Christ is counting on to introduce people to the Great Physician. Jesus is the one who saves the lost, but He needs our help. We are his hands and his feet. We may be the only Jesus some people see.

We Must Go Because Eternity is at Stake

Jesus is the one who said, "He that believes and is baptized shall be saved" (Mark 16:16). Jesus is also the one who said, "He who does not believe will be condemned. The KJV says, "damned."

I believe Jesus knew what he was talking about. If anyone knew how to get into heaven it was Jesus. If Jesus has commissioned us to go preach (announce, tell, declare, etc.) and we don't do it, should we be allowed into heaven? We must go preach because our soul and the souls of the lost are at stake.

CONCLUSION

We must go preach because it is the Gospel that has the power to save everyone who believes (Romans 1:16). I want you to think back over all these lessons on service from Mark's gospel. Many of you serve in some capacity in your church and in your community. Right now I want you to think of some way you can continue to serve the Lord. Jesus did not come into this world to be served but to serve, and to give His life as a ransom for many (Mark 10:45). We need to serve because that gives us credibility when we go to the lost. The key word in the gospel of Mark is "Servant". Let's go preach and serve!

A student went away to university. He partied, spent time on the computer and did just about everything but study. Soon he was flunking 4 of his 5 classes. He lost most of his friends and the ones he had were only superficial. He came to his senses and realized he needed to start walking with the Lord whom he had abandoned. He called his parents and told them that he had blown it academically, socially, and spiritually. His parents listened to all he had to say as he poured out his heart and soul. Then his parents said just three words. They weren't "We love you." They were better than that to this failing college student. They were, "Just come Home."

This is the message that we need to take to the lost, "Just come home!" Our God is in the reconciliation and reclamation business. He forgives and saves. Nothing is more important to Him than saving the lost. That is why we need to go preach.

Luke 15 tells us that there is great joy in heaven among the angels when a sinner repents.

Discussion Questions

1. Why is it important to go preach and win souls?

2. What does the word "preach" mean to you and who is to go and preach?

3. What three examples does Luke 15 give us that emphasizes the value of something that is lost?

4. What does Jesus say about baptism?

5. If we don't go and preach do you think we should be allowed in heaven?

6. Why did Jesus come into this world according to Mark 10:45?

7. Are you ready to go home?

Epilogue

Congratulations! You have finished this book. I hope you can look back on your study and say that you have learned what it means to be a servant. Now, apply what you have learned and go serve!

Mark learned what it meant to be a servant. He learned from some amazing guys like Peter, Paul, Barnabas and Jesus. I believe Mark understood the words of Peter in 1 Peter 1:21, "For you have been called for this purpose, since Christ also suffered for you, leaving you an example for you to follow in His steps."

Will you follow in the steps of Jesus and be a servant? If you serve the Lord and are faithful in living for Jesus you will hear the words every servant longs to hear, "Well done, good and faithful servant. You were faithful with a few things, I will put you in charge of many things; enter into the joy of your master" (Matthew 25:21).

Because of Christ, I am His humble servant!

Kim Huffman

Printed in the United States
By Bookmasters